LEON

BIG FLAVOURS

SALTY · SOUR · SPICY · SWEET

BY REBECCA SEAL

conran
OCTOPUS

First published in Great Britain in 2025
by Conran Octopus, an imprint of
Octopus Publishing Group Ltd
Carmelite House, 50 Victoria Embankment
London EC4Y 0DZ
www.octopusbooks.co.uk

An Hachette UK Company
www.hachette.co.uk

The authorised representative in the EEA is
Hachette Ireland, 8 Castlecourt Centre, Castleknock Road,
Castleknock, Dublin 15, D15 YF6A, Ireland

Distributed in the US by Hachette Book Group
1290 Avenue of the Americas
4th and 5th Floors, New York, NY 10104

Distributed in Canada by Canadian Manda Group
664 Annette Street, Toronto, Ontario, Canada M6S 2C8

ISBN 978-1-84091-826-7

A CIP catalogue record for this book is available from the
British Library.

Printed and bound in China.

10 9 8 7 6 5 4 3 2 1

Photography by Steven Joyce

Publishing director: Alison Starling
Creative director: Jonathan Christie
Senior developmental editor: Pauline Bache
Copyeditor: Patricia Burgess
Proofreader: Susan Low
Senior production manager: Katherine Hockley

Food styling: Troy Willis
Food styling assistant: Jess Geddes
Prop styling: Rosie Jenkins
Photography assistants: Rosie Alsop, Jordan Peck and
Dimitrios Brouzioutis

Key

WF — WHEAT FREE

GF — GLUTEN FREE

DF — DAIRY FREE

Ve — VEGAN

V — VEGETARIAN

NF — NUT FREE

SoF — SOY FREE

SUITABLE FOR FREEZING

SALTY   SOUR   SPICY   SWEET

Contents

Introduction

When we opened our first LEON in 2004, we had a simple mission: to challenge the idea that fast food couldn't be good food. Our founders were fed up with the bland options available to time-poor people, and set out to create meals that not only taste great but also do good for your body and mind.

Everyone at LEON is a bit of a food fanatic (seriously, get us started on our favourite restaurants and you'll need an escape plan). Our development team spends hours every week researching global flavours for our menus. We believe that your breakfast on-the-go or quick lunch between meetings should be lip-smackingly outstanding, and nutritious.

From the smoky paprika-spiked Red Shakshuka on our breakfast menu to the spicy-sweet gochujang in our Crunchy Korean Wrap, we're all about packing a punch with our flavours. This obsession and curiosity about bold tastes inspired us to compile our favourite recipes into this cookbook. We say this every time, but we really think this one's a corker, it may even be the best yet.

As you flip through these pages, keep an eye out for Rebecca's clever little flavour markers – they're your roadmap to the different tastes. And finally, a huge thank you for grabbing this book. We hope it becomes a dog-eared, sauce-splattered staple in your kitchen.

← Yoghurt & Herb Potato Salad *page 53*
Grilled Corn Salad *page 52*

BREAKFAST

Four Ways with Porridge

Porridge is a big deal at LEON, and we like to think it helps a lot of people to start their day happy.

SoF / NF / WF / GF / V • SERVES 1

- 50g (1¾oz) porridge oats (GF if needed)
- about 200ml (7fl oz) milk (DF, NF or SoF if needed)

1. For the basic porridge, place the oats in a small pan and add the milk. Set over a medium–low heat and cook, stirring, until done to your liking – we love it smooth, soft and creamy.

Blood Orange Curd & Chocolate Hazelnut

SoF / WF / GF / V

- 2 teaspoons hazelnut chocolate spread
- 1–2 teaspoons blood orange curd (we use Tiptree)
- 3 slices fresh orange, peel removed, or 3 segments canned mandarins
- a pinch of cacao nibs or grated dark chocolate, to garnish

This is based on a special porridge that we serve in the restaurants at Christmas. Place the hot porridge in a bowl, then swirl in the chocolate spread and orange curd. Add the fresh or canned orange pieces and sprinkle or grate over the cacao or chocolate. Eat immediately.

Peanut Butter, Sea Salt & Honey

SoF / WF / GF / V

- 2 teaspoons peanut butter
- 1–2 teaspoons honey
- flaky sea salt

Swirl the peanut butter and honey into the porridge, then finish with a little pinch of salt.

3

Miso & Maple Syrup

NF / WF / GF / V

- ½ teaspoon miso paste
- maple syrup, to taste

Mash the miso paste into the hot porridge until completely combined, then drizzle over a little maple syrup.

4

Sour Compote

SoF / NF / WF / GF / V

- 3 tablespoons frozen berries (not strawberries, as they tend to be mushy)
- pinch of soft dark brown sugar

Heat the berries, either in a small pan with a splash of water, or in a covered bowl in the microwave for a minute or so. Spoon them over the porridge and sprinkle over a good pinch of brown sugar. (This is also great with a swirl of nut butter.)

Berry Smoothie

We used to serve a smoothie very similar to this one in our restaurants, but with the addition of acai berries (which are quite hard to find in the shops). It's delicious with or without them, and full of goodness too.

PREP TIME 5 MINUTES • COOK TIME 0 MINUTES

SoF / NF / WF / GF / DF / V / Ve • SERVES 4

- 75g (2¾oz) frozen strawberries
- 125g (4½oz) frozen raspberries
- 50g (1¾oz) frozen blueberries
- 2 bananas
- 300ml (10fl oz) apple juice

1. Place all the ingredients in a blender and blitz until completely smooth.
2. Serve in tall glasses. Any leftovers, if covered, will keep in the fridge for a couple of days.

TIP

We have yet to find a fruit that you can't smoothify (answers on a postcard if you have) – melons, peaches, kiwis, cherries, pineapples... All good.

Avocado & Crispy Halloumi
English Muffins

Another of our breakfast-menu favourites.

PREP TIME 15 MINUTES • COOK TIME 6 MINUTES
SoF / NF • SERVES 4

- 2 avocados
- freshly squeezed lemon juice
- olive oil, for cooking
- 12 slices halloumi cheese
- 4 English muffins
- butter (optional)
- chilli sauce
- freshly ground black pepper
- lemon wedges, to serve

1. Scoop the avocado flesh into a bowl and roughly mash with a fork. Squeeze in a little lemon juice, mix and then taste to decide if you'd like more.

2. Place a frying pan over a medium heat, add a splash of olive oil and swirl it around the pan. Pat the halloumi dry with kitchen paper, then place the slices in the hot pan. Fry for about 3 minutes on each side, or until golden all over.

3. Split open and lightly toast the muffins, then spread one half of each muffin with butter, if using. Spread the other half with a quarter of the mashed avocado. Add the halloumi, season with pepper and add a splash of chilli sauce. Top with the other half of the muffin and serve immediately, with a wedge of lemon on each plate.

TIP

These are also great with a fried or poached egg instead of the cheese. Or try adding some pomegranate seeds for pops of sour sweetness and throw in a handful of your favourite fresh green herbs for even more flavour.

Hot Smoked Salmon & Avocado
English Muffins

Our avocado and salmon pots, but in a muffin.

PREP TIME 15 MINUTES • COOK TIME 5 MINUTES
SoF / NF • SERVES 4

- 2 avocados
- freshly squeezed lemon juice, to taste
- 100g (3½oz) hot-smoked salmon (or smoked mackerel)
- 4 eggs
- 4 English muffins
- butter (optional)
- salt and freshly ground black pepper
- lemon wedges, to serve

1. Scoop the avocado flesh into a bowl and roughly mash with a fork. Squeeze in a little lemon juice, mix and then taste to decide if you'd like more.

2. Warm the smoked fish, either briefly in the microwave or in a small pan with a dash of water to prevent it drying out.

3. For neat poached eggs, sieve the raw eggs before cooking and discard the loose runny white that falls through the sieve. Set a large pan of boiling water over a medium heat and bring to a simmer. Add another squeeze of lemon juice, then use a spoon to gently add the sieved eggs one at a time. They should then cook without lots of trailing white. (This works better than adding vinegar to the cooking liquid, we reckon.) Poach the eggs for about 4 minutes, or until done to your liking, then scoop them out with a slotted spoon and drain on a plate lined with kitchen paper.

4. Split open and lightly toast the muffins, then spread one toasted half of each muffin with butter, if using. Spread the other half with a quarter of the mashed avocado. Top the avocado with the warmed fish and a poached egg. Season with salt and pepper, then top with the other half of the muffin. Serve immediately, with a wedge of lemon on each plate.

Okonomiyaki

This is our favourite at-home version of a Japanese dish, which is made in different ways all over the country so there is no so there is no one set recipe. If you love the nutty flavour of toasted sesame oil, you can add a teaspoon of it to the batter, and a pinch of toasted sesame seeds to the garnish.

PREP TIME 15 MINUTES • COOK TIME 12 MINUTES

NF / V • SERVES 2 AS A LIGHT MEAL, OR 1 AS A MAIN MEAL

- 3 eggs, beaten
- 3 tablespoons plain flour
- 1 teaspoon cornflour
- a generous pinch of brown sugar
- ¼ teaspoon fine salt
- 1 teaspoon soy sauce
- 3 tablespoons water
- 150g (5½oz) white cabbage or hispi, or a mixture of both, finely shredded into small pieces
- 2 spring onions, green and white parts separated, both finely chopped
- 2 tablespoons neutral oil, for cooking

FOR THE SAUCES:
- 2 tablespoons mayonnaise
- 1 teaspoon soy sauce
- 1 teaspoon Henderson's Relish
- 2 tablespoons tomato ketchup
- 1 tablespoon soy sauce
- a pinch of sugar

TO GARNISH:
- sliced pickled ginger, crispy fried onions

1. Place the eggs, flour, cornflour, sugar, salt, soy sauce and water in a large bowl and beat together just until smooth (overmixing can make the batter gluey). Add the cabbage and white parts of the spring onion and mix well.

2. Set a 20cm (8in) frying pan over a medium heat. When hot, add the oil and tilt the pan to ensure the whole base is well coated. Pour the batter into the pan, and shape it into a thick fritter, using a spatula to pat the edges until neat. Cook gently for about 5 minutes, or until the base is golden and the pancake is set enough to turn over. Either use an extra-wide spatula to turn the whole pancake, or invert it onto a plate before sliding it back into the pan, uncooked-side down.

3. While the pancake is cooking, mix the mayonnaise and soy sauce together in a small bowl. In another small bowl, mix together the Henderson's Relish, ketchup, soy sauce and sugar. If you have squeezy bottles, transfer the sauces to them.

4. Once the pancake is golden on both sides, slide or lift it onto a plate. Zigzag the sauces over the pancake and sprinkle with the spring onion greens, pickled ginger and crispy onions to serve.

Green Shakshuka

A version of the super green shakshuka we serve in our breakfast boxes and pots.

PREP TIME 10 MINUTES • COOK TIME 18 MINUTES

SoF / NF / WF / GF / V • SERVES 4

- 5 tablespoons olive oil
- 1 red onion, finely chopped
- 3 cloves of garlic, crushed
- 1 large courgette, finely chopped
- 3 tablespoons finely chopped green chilli
- ½ teaspoon ground cumin
- 100g (3½oz) baby spinach (still wet from washing)
- 100g (3½oz) curly kale, chopped (still wet from washing)
- 12 slices halloumi cheese
- 4 eggs
- sea salt and freshly ground black pepper
- a handful of flat leaf parsley, chopped, to serve

1. Pour 2 tablespoons of the olive oil into a large frying pan and place over a medium heat. Add the onion and cook for 5 minutes, stirring often. Add the garlic and a good twist of salt and pepper, stir and cover with a lid. Turn the heat to low and cook for 5 minutes.

2. Add another tablespoon olive oil to the onion pan along with the courgette and chilli. Turn the heat back to medium and sauté without a lid for another 5 minutes, or until the courgette begins to soften. Add the cumin, spinach and kale and continue to sauté until the greens wilt right down. As they do so, the onions and garlic will begin to disintegrate.

3. Heat the oven to its lowest setting. Transfer the shakshuka to a bowl and keep warm in the oven. Wipe out the pan with kitchen paper and add another tablespoon oil. Fry the halloumi slices until lightly browned and keep warm, then fry the eggs in the remaining oil.

4. To serve, divide the shakshuka between four plates and top each serving with three slices of halloumi and a fried egg. Sprinkle over some parsley and eat straight away.

Erica's Baked Eggs

Erica Molyneaux is LEON's director of food, and this recipe is based on a dish once served at her former local, the Pigeonhole Café in Camberwell, south London, now sadly closed. She often recreates it at home for a weekend brunch.

PREP TIME 10 MINUTES • COOK TIME 25 MINUTES

SoF / NF / V • SERVES 2

- a generous knob of butter
- 1 small onion, finely sliced
- 2 cloves of garlic, finely sliced
- 400g (14oz) good-quality tomato passata
- ½ teaspoon chilli flakes
- a big handful of seasonal leafy greens (kale, spring greens or spinach), roughly chopped
- 4 eggs
- 6 tablespoons double cream or 3 tablespoons crème fraîche
- zest of ½ small unwaxed lemon (see Tip, page 82)
- salt and freshly ground black pepper

TO SERVE:
- Parmesan cheese (check V, if needed)
- buttered toasted sourdough

1. Place a wide ovenproof pan over a low heat and add the butter. When melted, add the onion and garlic and allow to soften, stirring often. Add the passata, chilli flakes and some salt and pepper, then simmer for 10–15 minutes, or until thickened.

2. Heat the oven to 200°C/425°F/gas mark 7.

3. Stir in the greens then make four dents in the mixture with the back of a spoon and break an egg into each one. Season each egg with a little salt and pepper, then drizzle the cream over the dish, or dot with the crème fraîche. Bake for 7–9 minutes, but check after 5 minutes, and keep checking, to see if the eggs have set to your liking – we prefer firm whites and runny yolks. How fast they cook depends on the thickness and depth of your pan and how hot the sauce was when it went into the oven.

4. Sprinkle the dish with the lemon zest and shavings of Parmesan. Serve with toasted sourdough.

TIP

You could swap out the cream/ crème fraîche for crumbled feta cheese (or use both), baked on top of the eggs, along with a pinch of ground cumin added to the passata. (Leave out the Parmesan.)

Crab Omelette

This is inspired by Tomos Parry's famous spider crab omelette, as served at his Soho restaurant, Mountain. If you can't find dried kelp (available online and in Japanese stores), toast a sheet of nori in a dry pan for 30 seconds and finely crumble by hand or in a spice grinder.

PREP TIME 10 MINUTES • COOK TIME 6 MINUTES

SoF / NF / WF / GF • SERVES 1–2, DEPENDING ON APPETITE

- 2 heaped tablespoons brown and white crab meat, at room temperature
- 3 eggs (ideally with golden yolks), plus 1 extra egg yolk
- 2 tablespoons butter
- fine sea salt

FOR THE SEAWEED BUTTER:
- 1 small piece of kombu or dried kelp, about 3 × 5cm (1¼ × 2in)
- 75g (2¾oz) soft butter

1. First make the seaweed butter. Place the seaweed in a mug and cover with boiling water. Leave for 5 minutes, until soft, then drain (keep the water to use as dashi stock, if you like). When cool, chop as finely as possible and mix three-quarters of it with the butter. Set aside. Mix the remaining chopped seaweed with the crab meat.

2. Put the eggs and extra yolk in a bowl with a generous pinch of salt and beat until the egg turns frothy. Add a spoonful of the egg mixture to the crab and mix well.

3. Place a dry 20cm (8in) frying pan over a medium heat. Once hot, turn the heat to low, add the 2 tablespoons butter and swirl it around the pan; then, working swiftly, pour in the beaten eggs. Stir briskly with a rubber spatula, as though scrambling them, and lifting the edges to let the unset mixture run underneath, smoothing out the omelette on top as you go. The goal is to set the underside of the eggs without browning, while the top remains loose and creamy. As soon as the base is mostly set, remove the pan from the heat and dot the omelette with the crab meat mixture. Fold the omelette into thirds to enclose the filling.

4. Slide the omelette onto a warm plate and melt a knob of the seaweed butter on top. Eat straight away.

TIP
The umami-rich leftover butter can be wrapped in clingfilm and stored in the fridge or freezer, ready to melt over grilled or roasted fish.

Miso-Garlic Mushrooms on Toast

Pile 'em high. (On toast.)

PREP TIME 10 MINUTES • COOK TIME 15 MINUTES

NF / V • SERVES 4

- 4 tablespoons neutral oil
- 400g (14oz) chestnut, mixed or wild mushrooms, trimmed and roughly chopped
- 3 tablespoons butter
- 2 cloves of garlic, crushed
- 1 tablespoon white miso paste
- 3 tablespoons single or double cream
- a pinch of chilli flakes (optional)
- 4 eggs
- 4 thick slices of bread (sourdough is great for this), toasted and buttered
- 2 tablespoons finely chopped chives
- freshly ground black pepper

1. Pour 2 tablespoons of the oil into a wide frying pan set over a medium–high heat. When hot, add the mushrooms and sauté until they begin to turn golden (if your pan is small, you will need to do this in batches, or they will boil in their own juices rather than caramelizing). When almost ready, add the butter and garlic to the pan and sauté for a further minute. Add the miso paste and a splash of water and cook, again stirring often, dissolving the miso. Add the cream, chilli flakes, if using, and some black pepper, then gently simmer until everything is saucy but not wet. Transfer the mushrooms to a bowl and keep warm.

2. Wipe out the pan and add the remaining 2 tablespoons oil. Place over a high heat and, when hot, fry the eggs quickly in order to get frazzled crispy edges.

3. Spoon the creamy mushrooms over the hot toast and top with a fried egg and the chopped chives.

Breakfast Fritters
with Avocado & Salsa

These crispy, veg-packed fritters have a fabulous sour-chilli kick, so if you're not a fan of heat, or if you're making them for kids, lower the quantity of jalapeños or just omit. This recipe is from a long list of ideas we've had over the years for our breakfast menu.

PREP TIME 20 MINUTES • COOK TIME 20 MINUTES

SoF / NF / WF / GF / DF / V • SERVES 4

- 100g (3½oz) frozen sweetcorn, defrosted
- 200g (7oz) sweet potato, grated
- 1 carrot, grated
- 3 tablespoons finely diced pickled jalapeños
- 2 spring onions, finely chopped
- a small handful of coriander leaves, finely chopped
- 2cm (¾in) piece of ginger, finely grated
- 2 cloves of garlic, crushed
- 1 teaspoon nigella seeds
- 2 teaspoons freshly squeezed lime juice
- 1½ teaspoons flaky sea salt
- zest of ½ unwaxed lime
- 1 teaspoon baking powder
- 85g (3oz) gram/chickpea flour
- neutral or olive oil, for cooking

FOR THE SALSA:
- a handful of coriander leaves, chopped
- 1 tablespoon finely chopped red chilli
- 1 tablespoon finely chopped shallot
- 150g (5½oz) cherry tomatoes, seeded, chopped
- ½ teaspoon red wine vinegar
- juice of ½ lime

TO SERVE:
- 4 eggs
- ½ avocado, diced
- hot sauce (optional)

1. Mix together all but the last three fritter ingredients. Add the baking powder and flour and stir again.
2. Combine all the salsa ingredients in a bowl with a pinch of salt.
3. Heat the oven to its lowest setting.
4. Pour a 5mm depth of oil into a wide frying pan over a high heat. Once the oil is hot, add 3 separate tablespoons of the batter to the pan, and press them into rounds about 7cm (2¾in) wide and just over 1cm (½in) thick. Don't make them too thick or the middle will be soggy. Fry without moving them – they will be fragile – for 4–5 minutes, or until golden brown on the base. Carefully turn each one – you might want to use two spatulas – and cook the other side until golden brown as well. Transfer to a plate lined with kitchen paper and keep warm in the oven. Make more fritters in the same way, adding more oil to the pan as needed. The mixture should make at least 12 fritters.
5. Once the fritters are made, fry the eggs in a little extra oil in the empty fritter pan.
6. Serve the fritters on warmed plates, with the eggs on top, the salsa alongside, the avocado scattered over and the hot sauce separately for those who want a little more heat.

Poached Eggs

with Watercress & Lemon-Truffle Mayo

Yes, it is a bit fancy to start the day with truffle mayonnaise. No, that's not going to stop us.

PREP TIME 12 MINUTES • **COOK TIME 8 MINUTES**

SoF / NF / V • **SERVES 2**

- 3 tablespoons mayonnaise
- freshly squeezed lemon juice, to taste
- extra-virgin olive oil
- truffle oil, ideally made with real truffles, to taste
- 4 big handfuls of watercress, thick stalks discarded, or use spinach, or a mixture of spinach and watercress
- butter, as needed
- 4 eggs
- salt and freshly ground black pepper
- 2 English muffins, or 2–4 slices of sourdough, toasted and buttered, to serve

1. Place the mayo in a bowl with a squeeze of lemon, a teaspoon of olive oil and another of truffle oil. Mix together, then taste, adding more lemon juice or truffle oil, as needed. Set aside.

2. Place the watercress or spinach in a small pan over a medium heat and add a splash of water. Cover with a lid and steam until completely wilted. Drain, squeezing out the excess water, then return it to the pan with a knob of butter, some salt and pepper and a squeeze of lemon juice.

3. For neat poached eggs, sieve the raw eggs before cooking and discard the loose runny white that falls through the sieve. Set a large pan of boiling water over a medium heat and bring to a simmer. Add another squeeze of lemon juice, then use a spoon to gently add the sieved eggs one at a time. They should then cook without lots of trailing white. (This works better than adding vinegar to the cooking liquid, we reckon.) Poach the eggs for about 4 minutes, or until done to your liking, then scoop them out with a slotted spoon and drain on a plate lined with kitchen paper.

4. Top each buttered muffin half with some of the watercress and a poached egg. Spoon over a little of the truffle mayo, then finish with a twist of black pepper.

2

SNACKY BITS

Goats' Cheese Filo Spirals
with Tzatziki

Rebecca has been cooking these since she tasted a similar pie, aged 19, on the Greek island of Alonissos. Use good-quality filo pastry, ideally from a Turkish or Middle Eastern grocers.

PREP TIME 20 MINUTES • COOK TIME 20 MINUTES

SPIRALS: SoF / NF / V • MAKES 6

TZATZIKI: WF / GF / V (CAN ALSO BE SoF / NF / DF / Ve, DEPENDING ON YOGHURT USED)

- 250g (9oz) soft rindless goats' cheese
- olive oil, for cooking
- 1 packet filo pastry (at least 6 sheets)

FOR THE TZATZIKI:
- ½ cucumber
- 1 clove of garlic, crushed to a paste
- 1 tablespoon finely chopped fresh dill
- 200ml (7fl oz) full-fat Greek-style yoghurt (SoF / NF / DF / Ve if needed)
- lemon juice, to taste
- 1 tablespoon extra-virgin olive oil
- paprika, for sprinkling
- salt and freshly ground black pepper

TO SERVE:
- salad of cucumber, tomato, red onion and parsley with extra-virgin olive oil

1. Mash the goats' cheese in a small bowl until soft and pliable.

2. Pour a 3cm (1¼in) depth of olive oil into a wide frying pan over a medium heat. While it's heating, make the spirals.

3. Remove one sheet of filo from the packet, covering the remainder with a damp tea towel. Lay the filo on a board and fold it in half lengthways, forming a rectangle about 30cm (12in) long and 18cm (7in) wide. Take about 40g (1½oz) of the cheese and spread it in a long line down the middle of the pastry, stopping about 3cm (1¼in) short of the ends. Roll up loosely to form a long tube. Gently pinch the ends of the tube together, then fold them over to seal. Coil the tube into a spiral and set aside. Make 5 more spirals in the same way.

4. When you've made all the spirals, place them in the hot oil, sitting the loose ends against the side of the pan so they can't unravel. Cook until the underside is golden, about 3–4 minutes, then carefully turn and cook the other side (by this point, the shape won't unravel). When crisp and golden brown, transfer to a plate lined with kitchen paper. Leave to cool for 5–10 minutes.

5. Meanwhile, make the tzatziki: grate the cucumber into a bowl, then squeeze out the excess liquid. Add the garlic, dill and yoghurt and mix well. Gradually add some lemon juice, olive oil and seasoning, tasting until you get your preferred flavour. Sprinkle with a pinch of paprika just before serving with the spirals and the salad.

Layered Feta & Pickled Chilli Filo Pie

This recipe is partly inspired by Mystik Burek, a brilliant Macedonian burek shop near Rebecca's house, and by gibinica, a beautiful layered filo, egg and cheese pie made throughout the Balkans.

PREP TIME 25 MINUTES • **COOK TIME 35 MINUTES**
SoF / NF / V • **SERVES 6–8**

- 2 tablespoons extra-virgin olive oil, plus extra for brushing
- about 12 sheets of filo pastry, depending on size
- 265g (9½oz) feta cheese, crumbled
- 100g (3½oz) cottage cheese
- 3 spring onions, finely chopped
- 4 long green pickled chillies, drained and finely chopped
- 4 eggs, beaten
- 2 tablespoons finely chopped dill
- a generous dusting of black pepper
- 2 teaspoons baking powder
- 2 tablespoons soured cream
- 150ml (5fl oz) sparkling water
- 1 teaspoon sesame seeds or nigella seeds, or a mixture

1. Brush the bottom and sides of a ceramic baking dish (roughly 20 × 24cm/8 × 9½in) with olive oil. Use 2 or 3 sheets of the filo to line the dish, overlapping them so there are no gaps and letting enough overhang the sides so that it can completely enclose the pie at the end.

2. Place the measured olive oil in a bowl and add all the remaining ingredients (apart from the water and seeds). Mix thoroughly, then stir in the water.

3. Heat the oven to 200°C/425°F/gas mark 7.

4. Take a sheet of the remaining filo and scrunch it up loosely into a ball. Dip it into the egg mixture for a moment, then lift out, using your hands and scooping up roughly two tablespoons of the mixture too. Tuck it into a corner of the lined dish. Repeat this step until the dish is full of crumpled pastry and egg mixture. Pour any remaining egg mixture over the pie.

5. Fold in the overhanging sheets of filo to completely cover the filling. Brush the pastry with more olive oil and sprinkle with the sesame or nigella seeds. Bake for 35 minutes, turning the dish around about 10 minutes before the end of cooking to ensure even browning.

6. Serve warm or at room temperature, with a herby salad or a sharp and crunchy slaw.

Sobrasada & Goats' Cheese Flatbreads

Sobrasada is a richly flavoured spreadable sausage from Majorca, with a flavour similar to that of Spanish chorizo (or 'nduja, which is Italian and a good stand-in). For this recipe, choose a spicy sobrasada or add some hot red chilli flakes.

PREP TIME 20 MINUTES • COOK TIME 12 MINUTES

PLUS 1 HOUR 20 MINUTES RISING

SoF / NF • SERVES 4–6

- 450g (1lb) strong white bread flour
- 50g (1¾oz) 'oo' flour or plain flour, plus extra for dusting
- 2½ teaspoons fast-action dried yeast
- 1 teaspoon sugar, any kind
- 2 teaspoons fine sea salt
- 2 tablespoons extra-virgin olive oil, plus extra for brushing
- 300ml (10fl oz) lukewarm water
- olive oil, for cooking

FOR THE TOPPING:
- about 125g (4½oz) spicy sobrasada or 'nduja, crumbled into 3cm (1¼in) chunks (see Tip opposite)
- 125g (4½oz) soft rindless goats' cheese
- about 100g (3½oz) rocket
- 4–5 tablespoons Pink Pickled Onions (see page 195 or use ready-made), chopped or sliced if large or chunky
- runny honey, for drizzling
- freshly squeezed lemon juice

1. Place all the flours and other dough ingredients (apart from the oil for cooking) in a large bowl, or stand mixer fitted with a dough hook. Mix together until a dough starts to form, then work with your hands to shape it into a smooth ball. If the mixture feels too dry and crumbly, add a splash of water, and if it feels too wet, a spoonful of flour.

2. Once the dough feels right, tip it onto a clean, lightly floured work surface and knead for 8–10 minutes by hand, or for 5 minutes in a mixer. It should feel elastic and silky. Return it to the bowl, cover with a damp tea towel and place somewhere warm for about 1 hour, until the dough has doubled in size.

3. Turn the dough onto a clean unfloured surface and squash it down to its original size. Twist it lightly – it will stick, but that's fine, as it allows tension to build up within it – then pull it off the surface and form into a neat, tight ball, again building up more tension. Divide into 6 equal pieces (about 125g/4½oz each) and roll into balls. Place on a floured tray or board, cover again with the damp tea towel, and leave to rise for about 20 minutes.

4. Heat the oven to its highest temperature and heat two metal baking trays in it.

5. When you're ready, take one piece of dough and stretch into a long flatbread about 14 × 22cm (5½ × 8½in), with a

narrow raised edge all around. Keep some of the air in it while shaping, and don't make it too thin – it's not meant to be like pizza. Brush the top all over with olive oil. Arrange one-sixth of the sobrasada and goats' cheese over the flatbread. Repeat to make all the flatbreads.

6. Remove the trays from the oven and brush with oil, then place three flatbreads on each one and bake for 10–12 minutes, or until puffed up and the sobrasada is melting and brown in places. .

7. Top each baked flatbread with a handful of rocket, a sprinkle of pink pickled onions, a drizzle of honey and a squeeze of lemon. Eat immediately.

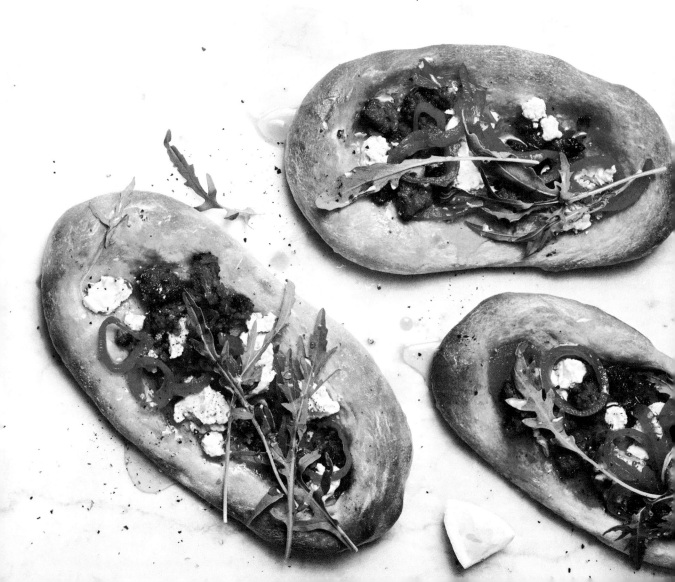

Pissaladière Tartlets

Pissaladière is traditionally a large French onion and anchovy tart, but the mini tartlets below work brilliantly as a starter with a little green salad, or they can go in your weekday lunch box. (If you want to make them bigger, increase the cooking time slightly.)

PREP TIME 20 MINUTES • COOK TIME 1 HOUR 35 MINUTES

SoF / NF • MAKES ABOUT 18

- 2 tablespoons butter
- 500g (1lb 2oz) onions
- a sprig of thyme
- 2 bay leaves
- a sprig of rosemary
- 3 cloves of garlic, peeled and whole, but bruised
- a pinch of salt
- 1 sheet ready-made shortcrust pastry
- 4 anchovies, very finely chopped
- 8 black olives, finely chopped
- 1 egg, beaten

1. Melt the butter in a heavy-based pan over a medium heat. Once bubbling, add the onions, herbs, garlic and salt. Stir just until the onions become translucent – no more than 5 minutes – then cover and cook very gently, stirring every 10 minutes or so, for 1 hour, by which point the onions should be pale gold and quite wet.

2. Take the pastry out of the fridge, let it come up to room temperature, and lay it on a clean work surface.

3. Remove the lid from the pan, increase the heat and let most of the liquid bubble away, allowing the onions to caramelize gently at the same time. Stir often to make sure they don't stick or burn. When done, they should be glossy-looking and silky soft. Remove and discard the garlic cloves (unless they've disintegrated) and the twiggy bits of the herbs. Take off the heat and stir in the anchovies and olives. (Normally they lie on top of a pissaladière, but in small pieces like this, they will burn in the oven.)

4. Heat the oven to 180°C/400°F/gas mark 6. Line a baking tray with nonstick baking paper.

5. Using an 8cm (3¼in) round cutter, stamp 18 circles out of the pastry and place them on the lined tray. Brush each one with beaten egg, then place a heaped tablespoonful of the onion mixture on top. Bake for 15–20 minutes, or until the pastry is golden both on top and underneath. Eat warm, or at room temperature.

TIP

If you don't like anchovies, or are vegetarian, replace both them and the olives with a little square of meltable cheese before putting in the oven, to make French onion soup-style tartlets instead.

Potato Bread Rolls
with Garlic & Anchovy Herbed Butter

Ever since Rebecca tasted a pillowy, sweet potato bread spiked with anchovy-and-herb butter several years ago, she has been on a mission to recreate it. This takes her straight back to that first bite.

PREP TIME 25 MINUTES + RISING/PROVING • COOK TIME 30 MINUTES

SoF / NF • MAKES 16

FOR THE DOUGH:

- 600g (1lb 5oz) strong white bread flour, plus extra for dusting
- 3 tablespoons caster sugar
- 2 teaspoons fast-action dried yeast
- 2 teaspoons fine sea salt
- 200g (7oz) smooth mashed potato
- 2 eggs, beaten
- 75g (2¾oz) butter, melted and cooled
- 150ml (5fl oz) warm water
- 1 egg yolk, to glaze

FOR THE ANCHOVY HERBED BUTTER:

- 125g (4½oz) unsalted butter, softened
- 3 cloves of garlic, crushed to a paste
- 6 anchovies, finely chopped and crushed to a paste
- a small handful of flat leaf parsley, very finely chopped
- a small handful of chives, very finely chopped
- a pinch of flaky sea salt

1. Place all the dough ingredients, except the separate egg yolk, in a bowl and mix together to form a dough, preferably with a dough hook as the mixture is sticky. Once combined, knead it lightly in the bowl. Place in a clean bowl, cover with a damp tea towel and leave in a warm place to rise for about 2 hours.

2. Line a 20 × 30cm (8 × 12in) baking tray with nonstick baking paper.

3. Tip the risen dough onto an unfloured surface and punch the air out of it. With a sharp knife, divide into 16 equal pieces. Shape them into tight balls by tucking all the ragged edges into a single point on the bottom of each ball, creating tension around the outside – it will be sticky, but don't add more flour. Arrange in rows on the baking tray, not quite touching. Place somewhere warm until doubled in size and touching each other. This might take 30 minutes, or an hour on a cold day.

4. Heat the oven to 180°C/400°F/gas mark 6. Whisk the remaining yolk with a tablespoon of water, then gently brush this glaze over each roll. Bake for 20–30 minutes, until golden and sounding hollow when tapped. Set aside to cool slightly.

5. Meanwhile, put all the butter ingredients, apart from the salt, into a bowl and mash until well combined.

6. To serve the rolls, use a serrated knife to make 2 or 3 incisions in the top of each one, going as deep as you can without cutting all the way through. Use a teaspoon to stuff the butter into the cuts, then brush or dot any remaining butter over the top. Finish with a pinch of flaky salt. Serve immediately.

Alicia's Gochujang Pancakes
with Sweet Gochujang Sauce

These Korean-style spiced pancakes are an excellent way to make the most of any vegetables in the fridge. Apart from those suggested below, you could add sliced sweet pepper, shredded cabbage or asparagus. (Thanks to Alicia Cooper, in our grocery team, for this one.)

PREP TIME 15 MINUTES • COOK TIME 20–30 MINUTES

NF / DF / V / Ve • SERVES 4

- 175g (6oz) plain flour (WF / GF if needed)
- 2 teaspoons baking powder
- 1 tablespoon cornflour
- 1½ teaspoons flaky sea salt
- 350ml (12fl oz) water
- 1 tablespoon gochujang (Korean chilli paste)
- 1 courgette, finely sliced into matchsticks
- 1 carrot, finely sliced into matchsticks
- 1 onion, halved and finely sliced
- 4 spring onions, trimmed and roughly chopped, plus 1 spring onion, finely sliced, to garnish
- 1 red chilli, finely chopped (optional)
- 2–3 tablespoons toasted sesame oil

FOR THE SWEET GOCHUJANG SAUCE:
- 4 tablespoons gochujang (Korean chilli paste)
- 2 tablespoons agave nectar or maple syrup (or honey if Ve not an issue)
- 2 teaspoons rice wine vinegar
- 1 tablespoon toasted sesame oil
- 1 clove of garlic, crushed to a paste (optional)

1. Place the flour, baking powder, cornflour and salt in a large bowl and stir to combine. Slowly add the water, whisking until you get a thick batter, then whisk in the gochujang until just combined – overmixing can make the batter gluey. Add the vegetables, mix once and set aside.

2. Whisk the sauce ingredients together in a bowl.

3. Place a large frying pan over a high heat. Add a tablespoon of the sesame oil and swirl it around to cover the bottom of the pan. Spoon in 2 or 3 mounds of the chunky batter (depending on the size of your pan) and smooth out to form separate pancakes about 10cm (4in) wide. (While it's possible to make 1 big pancake for each portion, they can be a bit harder to flip, so we like to make 2–3 smaller ones per person.) Cook briskly for 5 minutes, or until the base is crisp and golden – if they cook too slowly, the centre will be claggy. Flip and cook the other side in the same way. Transfer to a plate and keep warm while you make the rest of the pancakes, adding more oil each time.

4. Serve warm, garnished with the finely sliced spring onion and with small bowls of the dipping sauce on each plate.

Crispy Pickled Chillies
with Cheese

Our spicier, cheesier version of the now internet-famous deep-fried pickled gherkin (which have existed since the 1960s, but became famous on TikTok in the last couple of years).

PREP TIME 20 MINUTES • COOK TIME 20 MINUTES
SoF / NF / V • SERVES 4 AS A SNACK

- about 20 green chillies, pickled in brine
- neutral oil, for frying
- 125g (4½oz) soft rindless goats' cheese
- 1 tablespoon finely chopped chives
- 4 tablespoons plain flour, plus extra as needed (WF / GF if needed)
- 1 tablespoon cornflour, plus extra as needed
- 2 eggs, beaten
- about 100g (3½oz) panko breadcrumbs (or WF / GF alternative)

1. Line a plate with kitchen paper. Drain the pickled chillies, then cut a slit in them lengthways, starting about 1cm (½in) below the stem and finishing about 1cm (½in) from the tip. Allow any brine inside to spill out, then pat dry on the outside. Transfer to the prepared plate, cut-side down.

2. Place a high-sided frying pan or wide saucepan over a medium heat and add a 4cm (1½in) depth of cooking oil.

3. Place the cheese and chives in a small bowl and mash together.

4. Add the two flours to another small bowl and stir together. Place the eggs in a third bowl and the breadcrumbs in a fourth.

5. When the oil registers 175°C/345°F on a food thermometer, or a cube of day-old bread browns in 30 seconds when added to the hot oil, you can start frying.

6. Use a teaspoon to tuck a little of the cheese mixture inside each chilli, being sure not to overfill as they will expand during cooking. Press the chillies closed and dip first in the flour, then the egg (letting any excess drip back into the bowl). Then (to ensure they don't burst in the pan) dip them again in the flour and the egg, making sure they are completely coated. Finally, dip the chillies in the breadcrumbs, coating them thoroughly.

7. Use a slotted spoon to place 3 or 4 chillies at a time in the hot oil and cook for about 4 minutes, turning once, until golden. Drain on kitchen paper, and cook the rest of the chillies, letting the oil come back up to temperature between batches.

8. To eat, hold the stem and eat from the pointed end.

Kimchi Fritters
with Smacked Cucumber

Crispy, hot kimchi rice fritters with cool, sour cucumber. (Smacking cucumbers is fun and good for stress relief, but more importantly, bruising and partly crushing them helps them absorb other flavours while creating a soft-but-crunchy texture.)

PREP TIME 15 MINUTES • COOK TIME 20 MINUTES

NF / WF / GF / DF / V • SERVES 2

- 150g (5½oz) leftover cooked rice (or cook about 60g/2¼oz dry rice)
- 75g (2¾oz) frozen sweetcorn
- 1 small carrot, finely grated, liquid squeezed out
- 3 tablespoons finely chopped kimchi (shop-bought and V if needed, or see page 194 for homemade), liquid squeezed out
- 2 spring onions, finely chopped
- 2 eggs, beaten
- 1 tablespoon soy sauce (WF / GF if needed)
- 1 teaspoon paprika
- 2 tablespoons cornflour
- 1 teaspoon toasted sesame seeds
- neutral oil, for cooking

FOR THE CUCUMBER:
- ½ cucumber
- rice wine vinegar
- toasted sesame oil
- a pinch of salt, sugar and toasted sesame seeds

FOR THE DIPPING SAUCE:
- 1 tablespoon soy sauce (WF / GF if needed)
- 1 teaspoon rice wine vinegar
- 2 teaspoons water

1. Place the rice in a large bowl, add the sweetcorn, carrot, kimchi and spring onions and mix together. Add the beaten eggs, soy sauce and paprika and stir well. Finally, mix in the cornflour and sesame seeds.

2. Pour a thin layer of oil into a frying pan and place over a high heat. When hot, fry a nugget of the rice mixture for a couple of minutes, then taste for seasoning, adding more soy or paprika to the uncooked mixture if needed. Scoop a tablespoon of the mixture into the pan and flatten into a patty about 8cm (3¼in) wide and 2cm (¾in) thick. Fry 3 or 4 at a time, without moving them, for about 5 minutes, or until the underside is deep gold and crisp – if you flip too soon they will break apart. Cook the other side until deep gold too, then drain on a plate lined with kitchen paper. The mixture should make about 8 patties in all.

3. While the patties cook, gently bash the cucumber with a rolling pin on a wooden board until it splits open. Roughly chop all of the bashed cucumber into small pieces and place in a bowl, along with any juices that have escaped. Dress with a splash of rice vinegar and sesame oil, the salt, sugar and sesame seeds.

4. Stir together the dipping sauce ingredients in a bowl.

5. Serve the patties with the cucumber salad and a bowl of dipping sauce for each plate.

3

SOUPS
&
SALADS

Ollie's Roasted Cauliflower & Beetroot Salad

Ollie Short is one of our development chefs, and this very pretty salad is a recipe he regularly serves at home. The combination of the spiced roasted cauliflower and the tart pink dressing with pomegranate seeds is just perfect.

PREP TIME 15 MINUTES • COOK TIME 30 MINUTES

SoF / NF / WF / GF / DF / V / Ve • SERVES 4 WITH OTHER DISHES

- 1 head of cauliflower
- 3 tablespoons olive oil
- 1 tablespoon ground cumin
- 1 tablespoon ground coriander
- salt and freshly ground black pepper

FOR THE DRESSING:
- 50g (1¾oz) cooked beetroot (not pickled), roughly chopped
- 75g (2¾oz) coconut yoghurt (check SoF if needed)
- 2 teaspoons tahini
- 1 tablespoon fresh lemon juice
- 1 small clove of garlic, crushed
- a generous pinch of sea salt

FOR THE SALAD:
- 4 tablespoons Pink Pickled Onions (see page 195, or use ready-made)
- 4 tablespoons pomegranate seeds
- a generous pinch of sumac
- a handful of flat leaf parsley, roughly chopped
- a handful of mint leaves, roughly chopped

1. Heat the oven to 200°C/425°F/gas mark 7.
2. Slice off the cauliflower leaves, roughly chopping and reserving just the crisp ones. Break the cauliflower into florets and place in a large bowl. Add the olive oil and toss with your hands to ensure every piece is coated.
3. Combine the spices with a pinch of salt and lots of black pepper, then dust the cauliflower with the mixture, again tossing with your hands to ensure an even coating. Tip the cauliflower into a roasting tray and roast for 20 minutes.
4. Add the reserved leaves to the tray, tossing to coat lightly in the spices, and turn each piece of cauliflower. Return to the oven for a further 10 minutes, or until the cauliflower is tender and lightly charred in places. Set aside to cool to room temperature.
5. Meanwhile, using a blender, blitz the dressing ingredients together until smooth.
6. Serve the salad by arranging the cauliflower on a large plate. Spoon some of the beetroot dressing over it, then sprinkle with the pickled onions and pomegranate seeds. Add the sumac, and finish with the fresh herbs. Pour the remaining dressing into a jug and set it on the table.

Grilled Corn Salad

A great side for barbecues and grilled or roasted meats, such as the Carne Asada on page 161. If you want to eat it as a main, add some cooked and cooled black beans and maybe some finely chopped fresh red chilli too.

PREP TIME 10 MINUTES • **COOK TIME 10 MINUTES**

SoF / NF / WF / GF / V • **SERVES 4 AS A SIDE**

- neutral oil, for cooking
- 3 corn on the cob, outer leaves discarded
- 8 radishes, diced
- 3 spring onions, finely chopped
- 2 big handfuls of coriander, leaves only, roughly chopped,
- 200g (7oz) feta cheese, crumbled
- juice of 1 lime
- salt

1. Pour a splash of oil into a pan wide enough to fit all the corn cobs and place over a high heat. When hot, add the corn and cook, turning often, until golden in places and glossy all over. Set aside until cool enough to handle, then turn the cobs on end and slice off the kernels.

2. Place the corn in a bowl with the radishes, spring onions, coriander and feta. Squeeze the juice of half the lime over, plus a small pinch of salt. Stir, then taste and decide if it needs the rest of the lime – the salad should be tart, sweet from the corn and salty from the feta.

Yoghurt & Herb Potato Salad

While this is great as a side to grilled fish or chicken, it can be turned into
more of a main course if you sprinkle some crumbled feta and dried chilli over it,
or add chunks of smoked mackerel.

PREP TIME 10 MINUTES, PLUS COOLING • COOK TIME 15 MINUTES
SoF / NF / WF / GF / V • SERVES 4–6

- 500g (1lb 2oz) waxy potatoes, unpeeled
- 8 tablespoons Greek-style yoghurt (SoF / NF / DF / Ve if needed)
- 1 small clove of garlic, crushed to a paste
- 3cm (1¼in) piece of cucumber, very finely diced
- 2 tablespoons finely chopped dill
- 2 tablespoons finely chopped flat leaf parsley
- 2 tablespoons finely chopped chives
- 1 tablespoon freshly squeezed lemon juice
- 1 teaspoon wholegrain mustard
- 1 tablespoon extra-virgin olive oil
- salt and freshly ground black pepper

1. Cook the whole potatoes in a pan of boiling water for 12–15 minutes, until they are tender.
2. Meanwhile, combine all the other ingredients in a large bowl, adding a pinch of salt and lots of black pepper. The mixture should taste fresh and tart from the yoghurt and lemon. Add more lemon or salt, as needed.
3. Drain the potatoes and set aside until cool enough to handle. Chop into bite-sized pieces and add them, still warm, to the yoghurt mixture. Serve at room temperature, or chilled if you prefer, but remember that chilling will dim the flavours a little.

Sour & Salty Slaw

We've always had a slaw on LEON menus, and we love this tangy and sweet version. The basic recipe is very versatile, so we've also given a few dressing variations to go with different types of cuisine, or just to ring the changes.

PREP TIME 10 MINUTES • COOK TIME 0 MINUTES

SoF / NF / WF / GF / DF / V • SERVES 4–6

- 1 shallot, finely sliced
- 2 spring onions, finely chopped
- ½ red pepper, finely sliced
- ½ head of small white cabbage, finely sliced
- 1 carrot, finely sliced into matchsticks
- 75g (2¾oz) radishes, finely sliced into matchsticks
- 2 tablespoons finely chopped flat leaf parsley

FOR THE DRESSING:
- juice of ½ orange
- 1 tablespoon lemon juice
- 1 teaspoon runny honey
- 1 small clove of garlic, crushed
- ½ teaspoon fine salt
- 1½ teaspoons cider vinegar
- 2 tablespoons olive oil
- 2 tablespoons mayonnaise, or to taste (Ve, if needed)

1. Place all the vegetables and parsley in a large bowl.
2. Whisk the dressing ingredients together in a small bowl and taste – it should be salty, sour, a little sweet and very moreish. When you're happy with the flavour, pour it over the vegetables and mix well. Transfer to a serving dish. If the slaw has become wet, leave some of the excess dressing behind.

VARIATIONS TO TRY
- **Mexican-style:** omit the mayo and parsley, and instead add a squeeze of lime juice, some sliced red chilli and fresh coriander.
- **Indian-style:** omit the mayo, and add fresh coriander, ½ teaspoon freshly grated ginger, some chopped red chilli or chilli flakes, and some toasted cumin seeds.
- **Japanese-style:** omit the olive oil, orange juice and parsley, and add toasted sesame oil, a splash of soy sauce (WF / GF if needed) and a pinch of toasted sesame seeds to the dressing.
- **Fish dishes:** keep or omit the mayo, add finely chopped fresh dill and some toasted fennel seeds.
- **For grilled or smoky dishes:** add a pinch of smoked paprika if you like.
- **Try different vegetables:** add sliced fennel, green beans, peas, shredded beetroot, red cabbage or celeriac, and throw in a handful of nuts or toasted seeds.

Pan-fried Lettuce
with Anchovy Dressing

Turn this Caesar-inspired salad into a main course by adding a handful of crumbled blue cheese and some toasted nuts to each plate, or a jammy egg or two per person (boiled for 7½ minutes), or some leftover roast chicken.

PREP TIME 15 MINUTES • COOK TIME 8 MINUTES

SoF / NF / WF / GF • SERVES 4 AS A STARTER,

OR AS A MAIN WITH OTHER DISHES

- olive oil, for cooking
- 2 large heads of romaine lettuce, or 4 heads of little gem lettuce, cut into quarters
- Parmesan cheese, to serve

FOR THE DRESSING:
- 1 clove of garlic, crushed
- 3 anchovies in oil, drained and very finely chopped
- 1 tablespoon capers in brine, drained and roughly chopped
- 1 small shallot, very finely chopped
- 1 teaspoon finely chopped fresh dill
- 2 tablespoons finely chopped flat leaf parsley
- 1 teaspoon Dijon mustard
- 1 teaspoon sherry vinegar
- 1 teaspoon lemon juice
- 2 tablespoons extra-virgin olive oil
- 2 tablespoons mayonnaise
- 1–2 tablespoons cold water

1. Place all the dressing ingredients in a small bowl and mix thoroughly, then add enough cold water to make it just spoonable but not wet. Set aside.
2. Place a large frying pan over a medium–high heat. When hot, add a splash of cooking oil to the pan, then add the lettuce, cut-side down (you will probably need to work in batches). After a minute or so, check to see if the underside is browning. If so, gently turn the lettuce over and cook for 1 more minute.
3. Transfer the lettuce to a large serving platter or individual plates, browned-side up. Spoon over about half the dressing, then shave over some Parmesan. Serve warm, with the rest of the dressing at the table.

Chicken & Coconut-Curried Noodles

Warm your cockles with these fiery noodles, finished with fresh herbs and sour lime. With like this with rice noodles but, if there's no need to be GF or WF, egg noodles work too.

PREP TIME 20 MINUTES   **COOK TIME 18 MINUTES**

SoF / NF / WF / GF / DF   **SERVES 4**

- neutral oil, for cooking
- 1 × 400ml (14fl oz) can coconut milk
- 300ml (10fl oz) hot chicken stock
- 1 teaspoon dark brown sugar
- 2 lime leaves
- 4 chicken thighs, skinless and boneless, sliced into bite-sized pieces
- 100g (3½oz) bean sprouts
- 100g (3½oz) green beans, trimmed
- 200g (7oz) dried rice noodles

FOR THE SPICE PASTE:
- 1 stick of lemongrass, tough outer layer removed, roughly chopped
- 1½ tablespoons neutral oil
- ½ onion, roughly chopped
- 4cm (1½in) piece of ginger, peeled, chopped
- 3 cloves of garlic
- zest of 1 unwaxed lime (see page 82)
- 2 teaspoons ground turmeric
- ½ teaspoon fine salt
- 1 teaspoon each ground cumin and coriander
- 2–3 red chillies, roughly chopped
- 2 teaspoons chilli powder
- 2 teaspoons fish sauce, plus extra to taste

TO SERVE:
- lime wedges
- a handful of coriander leaves
- a handful of mint leaves
- 1 fresh red chilli, sliced on an angle
- 50g (1¾oz) cucumber, as matchsticks

1. Start by placing all the spice paste ingredients in a blender or food processor and blitzing until fairly smooth. You'll need to scrape down the sides once or twice.

2. Pour a splash of oil into a large, heavy-based saucepan over a medium heat. When hot, add the spice paste and fry gently, stirring frequently, until the paste separates and starts to look oily, about 5 minutes. Open the coconut milk and scoop some of the cream from the top into the paste. Stir and fry for 1 minute, then add the rest of coconut milk, the chicken stock, sugar and lime leaves and bring up to a simmer. Let bubble for 5 minutes. Add the chicken pieces and simmer until cooked through, about 8 minutes. Taste the broth and season with a splash of fish sauce, if needed.

3. While the broth cooks, set a pan of freshly boiled water over a high heat and bring to a simmer. Blanch the bean sprouts and green beans for 1 minute, then use tongs or a strainer to remove them. Set aside. Add the noodles to the same water and cook according to the packet instructions. Drain.

4. Divide the cooked noodles between four wide serving bowls. Spoon over the broth and the chicken, and add a portion of bean sprouts and green beans to each bowl. Top each serving with a lime wedge, some coriander and mint leaves, a sprinkling of red chilli and some cucumber sticks. Eat straight away.

Chana Masala Soup

A hug in a bowl, this warming soup features the humble chickpea, one of LEON's most-used ingredients. We love a legume.

PREP TIME 15 MINUTES • COOK TIME 40 MINUTES

SoF / NF / WF / GF / DF / V / Ve • SERVES 4

- ¼ red onion, finely sliced
- lime or lemon juice
- 2 tablespoons vegetable oil, for cooking
- 2 white onions, finely sliced
- 1 tablespoon mustard seeds
- 1 tablespoon cumin seeds
- 5cm (2in) piece of ginger, finely grated
- 4 cloves of garlic, crushed
- 6 curry leaves
- a pinch of dried fenugreek leaves
- 2 teaspoons ground coriander
- 1½ teaspoons garam masala
- 3 tablespoons finely chopped green chillies, or more to taste
- 1 × 400g (14oz) can chopped tomatoes or passata, or freshly skinned tomatoes in the summer
- 200ml (7fl oz) hot vegetable stock, plus more as needed
- 2 × 400g (14oz) cans chickpeas and their water
- a pinch of amchoor (dried mango) powder, or ½ teaspoon tamarind paste, from a jar
- salt

TO SERVE:
- squeeze of lemon juice
- warmed Indian flatbreads (WF / GF / DF / Ve if needed)

1. Place the red onion in a small bowl and squeeze over enough lime or lemon juice to coat. Set aside until ready to serve.

2. Place a large pan over a medium heat and add the oil. When hot, add the white onions and cook, stirring often, until beginning to brown; 6–8 minutes. Add the both lots of seeds and fry until the mustard seeds begin to crackle and pop. Now add the ginger, garlic, curry leaves, fenugreek, ground coriander, garam masala and fresh chillies. Cook on a low heat for 4–5 minutes, stirring so that the garlic and ginger don't stick and burn. Add the tomatoes, stock, chickpeas and their water and stir well to combine. Lower the heat to a simmer, cover the pan and cook gently for about 20 minutes. Check every now and then to make sure the pan isn't drying out, and add a splash more stock if needed. Add the amchoor powder or tamarind at the end of cooking.

3. Taste and decide if you want to add any more salt or green chilli. Remove from the heat and add a squeeze of lemon juice and some of the sliced red onion, just before serving.

Loaded Miso Soup

Traditionally, proper miso soup is made with miso paste, dashi (a stock made with kombu kelp and bonito), tofu cubes, seaweed and spring onion. This miso-only soup is spiked with crunchy radish, and the tofu is quickly pan-fried.

PREP TIME 15 MINUTES • COOK TIME 15 MINUTES

NF / WF / GF / DF / V / Ve • SERVES 2

- 200g (7oz) extra-firm tofu, cut into 2cm (¾in) cubes
- 3 tablespoons cornflour
- neutral oil, for cooking
- a pinch of dried wakame seaweed
- 700ml (1¼ pints) boiling water
- 1 tablespoon miso paste (WF / GF if needed)
- 7 radishes, finely sliced
- 3 spring onions, halved lengthwise and finely chopped

1. Place the cubed tofu in a bowl, sprinkle with the cornflour and toss to coat. Set a large frying pan over a medium heat. When hot, add a generous splash of oil, then add the tofu. Fry for about 4 minutes without moving it, or until golden on the bottom. Turn and fry the other sides, until golden and crunchy all over.

2. Meanwhile, place the wakame in a mug of hot water and set aside. Pour the boiling water into a large pan set over a medium heat. Whisk in the miso paste and bring to a simmer. Drain the wakame and add to the pan. Taste the broth, and add more miso if needed – it should be very savoury and quite salty.

3. Divide the broth between two bowls. Just before serving, add the radishes, spring onion and fried tofu. Eat straight away.

TIP

Optional extras or swaps for the tofu include: hard-boiled eggs seasoned with soy sauce, fried smoked mackerel fillets, greens, sautéd mushrooms, edamame beans, peas, or noodles cooked in the broth.

Erica's Harira Soup

Another winner from Erica, LEON's director of food – her version of a warming, gently spiced Moroccan soup-stew, finished with a swirl of harissa.

PREP TIME 20 MINUTES • COOK TIME 1¾ HOURS

SoF / NF / WF / GF • SERVES 4

- 2 tablespoons olive oil
- 1 large onion, finely chopped
- 3 cloves of garlic, finely chopped
- 3 carrots, finely chopped
- 2 celery sticks, finely chopped
- 2cm (¾in) piece of ginger, finely chopped
- 3 sprigs of flat leaf parsley, leaves picked, stalks finely chopped
- 600g (1lb 5oz) boneless leg or boneless shoulder of lamb
- 1 tablespoon ground cumin
- 1 tablespoon ground turmeric
- 1 heaped teaspoon ground cinnamon
- 1 heaped teaspoon ground coriander
- 3 bay leaves
- 1 tablespoon tomato purée
- 700ml (1¼ pints) hot vegetable stock
- 1 × 400g (14oz) can good-quality chopped tomatoes
- 1 × 400g (14oz) can chickpeas, plus their liquid
- salt and freshly ground black pepper

TO SERVE:
- plain live yoghurt (SoF / NF / DF if needed)
- 2 tablespoons harissa
- warmed flatbreads (WF / GF if needed)

1. Drizzle the olive oil into a large pan over a low–medium heat and sauté the chopped vegetables, ginger and parsley stalks for 10 minutes, until softened.
2. Meanwhile, trim the lamb of excess fat and cut the meat into 2–3cm (¾–1¼in) pieces.
3. Season the softened vegetables with salt and pepper, then add the lamb. Turn up the heat to brown the lamb, and cook for 5–7 minutes, stirring often.
4. Add the ground spices, the bay leaves and tomato purée, stir well and cook for a further 3 minutes. Add the stock, tomatoes, chickpeas and their liquid, stir well and bring to the boil. Lower the heat, cover with a lid and simmer for 1 hour.
5. Remove the lid and cook for a further 30 minutes, or until the meat is tender. (Add a bit of water if it gets a little too thick.)
6. Season to taste and portion into wide bowls. Serve with a dollop of the yoghurt, a swirl of harissa, a sprinkling of finely chopped parsley leaves and a warmed flatbread.

Smoked Mackerel Udon Broth
with Choi Sum

This simple, almost green-tasting udon soup isn't made with the usual miso or soy sauce. It gets most of its flavour from wakame seaweed and vegetables, plus the salty smoked fish.

PREP TIME 15 MINUTES • COOK TIME 20 MINUTES

NF / DF • SERVES 4

- 4 eggs
- 4 pinches dried wakame seaweed
- neutral oil, for frying
- 4 smoked mackerel fillets, skin removed, flesh broken into large pieces
- 1 teaspoon bouillon powder (or use homemade vegetable stock or very, very weak vegetable stock from a cube)
- 200g (7oz) choi sum (flowering cabbage), stems separated and roughly chopped
- 200g (7oz) dried udon noodles (WF / GF if needed)
- 12 spears of fine asparagus, halved lengthways
- 4 spring onions, sliced on an angle
- salt, if needed

1. Place a pan of freshly boiled water over a medium heat and bring to a simmer. Add the eggs and cook for 7 minutes, then transfer to a bowl of cold water. When cool enough to handle, peel and set aside.

2. Place the wakame in a mug of boiling water and set aside.

3. Set a frying pan over a medium heat and add a dash of oil. Add the mackerel pieces and fry for about 3 minutes on each side, until golden. Remove the pan from the heat.

4. Fill a large pan with about a litre (1¾ pints) of freshly boiled water and bring to a simmer. Add the bouillon powder, soaked and drained wakame, noodles and choi sum stems and simmer for about 5 minutes. Add the leaves and asparagus and cook for 2 minutes longer. Taste the broth and add a pinch of salt, if needed. When the stems and noodles are tender, divide between four bowls.

5. Cut the eggs in half and place them to one side of the broth, arranging the fish alongside. Sprinkle over the spring onions and eat straight away.

4

SIMPLE BUT MIGHTY

Leon Crispy Chicken & Gochujang Wrap

This is an at-home version of our much-loved LEON Crunchy Korean Chicken Wrap. We bake our chicken nuggets, but they can be shallow-fried for about 4 minutes a side if you prefer.

PREP TIME 15 MINUTES • COOK TIME 20 MINUTES

NF • SERVES 4

- 4 heaped tablespoons homemade Fermented Kimchi (see page 194), or an unpasteurized ready-made version (we like Eaten Alive), drained and chopped
- 1 small carrot, coarsely grated
- 40g (1½oz) shredded red cabbage
- 25g (1oz) shredded kale (2 large leaves)
- a handful of green beans, finely sliced
- 4 wraps (we use Khobez)

FOR THE GOCHUJANG MAYO:
- 2 tablespoons mayonnaise
- 2 teaspoons Greek-style yoghurt
- 1½ teaspoons gochujang (Korean chilli paste), or to taste
- fresh lime juice, to taste

FOR THE CHICKEN:
- neutral oil, for cooking
- plain flour, for dredging (WF / GF if needed)
- 2 eggs, beaten (or 5 tablespoons aquafaba, the water from a can of chickpeas, thickened if very thin by reducing on the hob)
- about 200g (7oz) ready-made breadcrumbs (WF / GF if needed)
- 4 boneless, skinless chicken thighs, cut into nugget-sized (4cm/1½in) pieces
- salt and freshly ground black pepper

1. Prepare the kimchi and all the vegetables. Whisk together the mayo ingredients.
2. Heat the oven to 200°C/425°F/gas mark 7. Generously grease a baking tray with the oil.
3. To make the nuggets, pour the flour into a small bowl, along with a good twist of salt and pepper; place the beaten eggs (or aquafaba) in another bowl; and tip about half the breadcrumbs into a third bowl. Dip each chicken piece first in the flour, then the egg and finally the crumbs, being sure to cover thoroughly in each coating (top up the crumb bowl as needed). Transfer to the prepared baking tray.
4. Bake the nuggets for 14 minutes, turning twice during cooking. When ready, they should be golden brown and very crisp, and the meat should be cooked through, with any juices running clear. Alternatively, cook in an air-fryer at 200°C/425°F for about 10 minutes, turning once halfway through.
5. Warm the wraps in a low oven for a couple of minutes. To assemble, place 3 nuggets on each wrap, then top with a handful of prepared vegetables and a spoonful of kimchi. Add a dollop of the gochujang mayo. Fold the bottom of each wrap over the filling, then turn the sides in and fold the top down. Serve immediately.

Mariam's Green Chutney Grilled Cheese Sandwich

Mariam French works at LEON HQ, and her family is originally from Kerala. Mariam is queen of condiments, and loves this coriander, coconut and chilli chutney in a toasted cheese sandwich. (She says this is particularly good if you've had a few glasses of wine the night before.)

PREP TIME 10 MINUTES • COOK TIME 5 MINUTES

SoF / NF / V • SERVES 1

- 2 slices of sourdough, or any other sturdy bread
- butter
- Cheddar cheese, grated

FOR THE CHUTNEY:
- 3 tablespoons desiccated coconut
- ¼ teaspoon fine salt
- leaves from a small sprig of mint
- a big handful of coriander, thick stalks removed, roughly chopped
- 1 green chilli, roughly chopped
- ½ small onion, roughly chopped
- juice of 1 small lemon

1. Place all the chutney ingredients in a blender or food processor, add a splash of water and blitz together.
2. To make the sandwich, butter the bread, then turn it over so the butter will be on the outside. Cover one slice with some of the cheese, then spoon over some of the chutney. Sprinkle over a little more cheese (this will melt and hold the sandwich together). Top with the other slice of bread.
3. Set a small frying pan over a medium heat and add the sandwich. Fry for 3–5 minutes on each side, or until golden brown all over and oozing with melted cheese.

TIP

Mariam's Spicy Bomb Sauce (see page 186) is also tremendously good in the melting middle of a grilled cheese sandwich.

Bangin' Bhaji Burgers

We serve a version of these gently spiced bhajis (baked rather than fried) wrapped in a flatbread, in our restaurants. You can't go wrong with a portion of chips or wedges on the side (or some LEON baked fries), but if you want even more veg on your plate, corn on the cob wouldn't go amiss.

PREP TIME 20 MINUTES • COOK TIME 35 MINUTES

SoF / NF / V • SERVES 4

FOR THE BHAJI:

- ½ red onion, finely sliced
- ½ courgette, finely diced
- 50g (1¾oz) broad beans
- 100g (3½oz) frozen peas
- 3 cloves of garlic, finely grated
- 6cm (2½in) piece of ginger, peeled and finely grated
- 1 tablespoon freshly squeezed lemon juice
- a big handful of coriander leaves, chopped
- a big handful of mint leaves, chopped
- 2 heaped teaspoons finely chopped jalapeño chillies, or more, to taste
- 2 teaspoons cumin seeds
- 2 teaspoons nigella seeds
- ½ teaspoon ground turmeric
- ¼ teaspoon chilli powder
- 120g (4¼oz) chickpea (gram) flour
- 2 tablespoons cornflour
- ½ teaspoon fine salt
- 100ml (3½fl oz) water
- neutral oil, for cooking

1. Place all the bhaji ingredients, except the oil, in a large bowl and mix well until you end up with a batter – there won't be much, but it will be enough to hold the bhaji together without being claggy.

2. Combine all the mayo ingredients in a separate bowl. Heat the oven to its lowest setting.

3. While bhajis can be shallow-fried, we love the crunch you get from deep-frying, so pour about 8cm (3¼in) cooking oil into a deep saucepan over a medium heat. When it registers about 175°C/345°F on a thermometer, or when a cube of bread added to the oil browns in about 30 seconds, it's ready to use. (If it's too hot, lower the heat.) Start by cooking just a little of the bhaji mixture for a couple of minutes in order to test the seasoning; taste and add more spice or heat to the batter if you like.

4. Place 3 separate tablespoons of the batter in the hot oil and leave to fry for about 6 minutes, or until golden, then carefully flip them over to cook the other side. After a couple more minutes, and once the bhajis are deep golden and very

FOR THE HERBED MAYO:

- 3 tablespoons mayonnaise (SoF / NF / Ve if needed)
- 3 tablespoons plain Greek-style yoghurt (SoF / NF / DF / Ve if needed)
- 2 tablespoons finely chopped mint leaves
- 2 tablespoons finely chopped coriander leaves
- 1 clove of garlic, crushed
- ¼ teaspoon nigella seeds

TO SERVE:

- 4 brioche burger buns (WF / GF if needed)
- garnishes, such as: crisp lettuce leaves, finely chopped cherry tomatoes and cucumber, Pink Pickled Onions (see page 195), crispy onions (from a packet), LEON mango ketchup (or 50:50 ketchup and mango chutney)

crisp, transfer them to a plate lined with kitchen paper to drain. Keep them warm in the oven while you cook the rest. You should have enough batter to make 12 bhajis.

5. To serve, split open and lightly toast the buns. Spread the bottom half of each one with the herbed mayo and the top half with mango ketchup. Stack 3 bhajis on top of the mayo, then add some lettuce, tomato, cucumber, Pink Pickled Onions and crispy onions. Top with the ketchup-covered halves and serve straight away, maybe with some fries and more mango ketchup on the side.

Black Bean Egg-Fried Rice

For Sundays when you got up too late for breakfast, or for WFH lunches when you need something to kick start your afternoon.

PREP TIME 15 MINUTES • COOK TIME 10 MINUTES

SoF / NF / WF / GF / V • SERVES 2

- 1 tablespoon neutral oil or mild olive oil
- about 250g (9oz) leftover cooked rice (or cook about 100g/3½oz dry rice)
- 1 red chilli, finely chopped (or more to taste)
- ½ red pepper, diced
- 100g (3½oz) frozen or canned sweetcorn, drained
- 1 spring onion, finely chopped
- 1 clove of garlic, crushed
- 1 × 400g (14oz) can black beans, drained and rinsed (or about 225g/8oz cooked black beans)
- ¼ teaspoon ground cumin
- ¼ teaspoon ground coriander
- 2 eggs, beaten
- 100g (3½oz) feta cheese, crumbled
- freshly ground black pepper

TO SERVE:
- coriander leaves
- lime juice
- hot sauce

1. Place a wide frying pan over a medium-high heat and add the oil. Tip everything apart from the eggs and cheese into the pan and sauté briskly, tossing well. Crack the eggs into the pan and continue to mix, scrambling them into the rice mixture. Remove from the heat, scatter over the feta and some black pepper, and mix gently, once only. (You probably won't need salt, as both the feta and hot sauce are salty.)

2. Divide between two warmed plates, then sprinkle with a few coriander leaves, a squeeze of lime juice and a splash of hot sauce. Eat straight away.

Marmite Pasta
with Crispy Crumbs & Egg Yolk

Nigella Lawson made Marmite pasta famous, but credits the Italian cookery writer Anna Del Conte with the idea. The original is a simple butter-and-Marmite emulsion, but we make it with egg yolk and toasted sourdough crumbs for a richer but still very quick meal.

PREP TIME 5 MINUTES • COOK TIME 15 MINUTES

SoF / NF / V • SERVES 2

- 200g (7oz) long pasta (spaghetti, linguine or tagliatelle)
- 40g (1½oz) butter
- 1 teaspoon Marmite
- 2 tablespoons finely grated Parmesan cheese (check V, if needed)
- 2 egg yolks, at room temperature (save the whites to make the meringues on page 210)
- freshly ground black pepper

FOR THE PANGRATTATO:
- 2 tablespoons extra-virgin olive oil
- 1 slice sourdough bread, torn or chopped into breadcrumbs
- fine salt

1. First make the pangrattato: place a small frying pan over a medium heat. Add the oil, then the breadcrumbs and toast, stirring often, until deep golden and very crisp, about 8–10 minutes. Season with a pinch of salt. Set aside.

2. Cook the pasta in a pan of boiling salted water, using a bit less water than usual to make it starchier. When al dente, or about 1 minute less than the packet suggests, scoop out a mugful of pasta water to use in the sauce, then drain the pasta and return it to the pan. Immediately add the butter, Marmite, Parmesan and 4 tablespoons of the pasta water and stir vigorously to form a light, silky sauce (if it seems dry, add another spoonful of cooking water). Taste. It should be slightly salty and very savoury; add more Marmite, if needed.

3. Divide the pasta and sauce between warmed pasta bowls and top each with a handful of the pangrattato. Make a little well in the centre of each portion and add an egg yolk. Grind a little pepper over each bowlful and serve straight away.

Spaghetti Alla Puttanesca

Could we write a book called 'Big Flavours' and not include a recipe for this intensely flavourful Roman pasta dish? We could not.

PREP TIME 10 MINUTES • COOK TIME 10 MINUTES

SoF / NF / DF • SERVES 4

- 400g (14oz) dried linguine or spaghetti (WF / GF if needed)
- 2 tablespoons extra-virgin olive oil
- 4 cloves of garlic, finely chopped
- 2½ tablespoons tomato purée
- 6 anchovies in oil, finely chopped
- 5 tomatoes, deseeded and finely chopped, or 200g (7oz) passata or crushed tomatoes from a can
- 3 tablespoons capers in brine, rinsed and roughly chopped
- 12 black or purple olives, pitted and roughly chopped
- a generous pinch of chilli flakes
- a handful of flat leaf parsley leaves, roughly chopped

1. Cook the pasta in a pan of boiling salted water until al dente. Drain, reserving half a mugful of the starchy pasta water.

2. While the pasta cooks, place the olive oil in a small frying pan over a medium heat. Add the garlic and sizzle gently for a minute or so, stirring to make sure it doesn't burn (turn the heat down if it cooks too quickly). Add the tomato purée and anchovies and cook for a couple of minutes longer, until the anchovies melt and the purée begins to smell more cooked than raw. Add the tomatoes, capers, olives and chilli flakes and cook for 3–4 minutes, stirring often, until the tomatoes begin to collapse (crush any lumps with the back of a spoon or a masher to hurry this stage along if needed). Add 2 tablespoons of the pasta water and stir well, adding more as needed to make a sauce that will cling to the pasta.

3. Stir the sauce into the pasta, along with the parsley leaves, and serve straight away.

TIP

Vegetarians and vegans can make this dish without the anchovies; add grated vegan Parmesan-style cheese at the end to make up the missing umami.

Pasta al Limone

In this classic Italian pasta dish, lemon is the star ingredient, with Parmesan melting into the zest to create a silky yet zingy sauce. And it all comes together in barely more than 10 minutes. (Be sure to use an unwaxed lemon for this one.)

PREP TIME 5 MINUTES • COOK TIME 7–8 MINUTES

SoF / NF / V • SERVES 4

- 400g (14oz) dried linguine
- 100g (3½oz) unsalted butter, chopped into small pieces
- 75g (2¾oz) freshly grated Parmesan cheese, plus extra to serve (check V, if needed)
- zest of 1 large unwaxed lemon (see Tip, below)
- sea salt

1. Bring a pan of salted water to the boil, using slightly less water than usual for pasta – this raises the level of starch in the water, which will be useful later. Add the pasta and cook until al dente, 7 minutes or so, or about 1–2 minutes less than the packet suggests.

2. Meanwhile, melt the butter in a small pan or in the microwave.

3. When the pasta is done, use a mug to scoop out about 150ml (5fl oz) of the cooking water and set it aside. Drain the pasta and return it to the hot pan, along with the melted butter, Parmesan, about half the lemon zest and a good pinch of salt. Use a wooden spoon to rapidly mix the pasta, allowing the butter and cheese to emulsify into a sauce around it. If the pan seems at all dry or claggy, add some of the reserved pasta water, just a tablespoonful at a time, until you have a light, silky sauce. (Don't let it get too wet.) Add a tablespoonful of lemon juice, then taste and season with more salt, lemon zest or Parmesan, as needed.

4. Divide between 4 wide, shallow bowls and serve with a little more Parmesan grated over each serving and a pinch of the remaining lemon zest.

TIP

If you can't find unwaxed citrus fruit, scrub the peel in hot water to remove any wax before using the zest.

Posh Noodle Pots

Instant noodles, plus a few extras, can make meals on the run so easy. Take one of these posh pots (and even a vacuum flask of freshly boiled water) with you any time you're on the go and you will always be certain of getting a decent lunch.

PREP TIME 15 MINUTES • COOK TIME 3 MINUTES

NF / DF • SERVES 1

- 1 heaped teaspoon miso paste
- small handful of edamame beans, defrosted if frozen
- 6 mangetout
- 1 spring onion, finely sliced
- 2 broccoli florets, finely sliced
- 1 head of pak choi, stems and leaves finely sliced
- 50g (1¾oz) instant noodles
- 25g (1oz) cooked and peeled cold-water prawns, or firm tofu, chopped into small cubes
- 3 thin slices of cucumber, cut into matchsticks
- 2cm (¾in) piece of red chilli, halved and roughly chopped
- 300ml (10fl oz) boiling water

FOR THE SAUCE:
- 1 tablespoon soy sauce
- 1 teaspoon sesame oil
- 1 teaspoon lime juice

1. Set out a 350–500ml (12–18fl oz) heatproof jar with a lid. Mix the miso with a splash of water (this is to make it easier to dissolve in the boiling water later). Add it to the jar, then add the edamame beans, mangetout, spring onion, broccoli and pak choi. Break up the noodles and add them to the jar in a single layer. Now add the prawns, cucumber and red chilli. Seal the jar and refrigerate until you want to eat.

2. Pour the soy sauce, sesame oil and lime juice into a small plastic pot or mini jam jar, cover with a lid and set aside until needed.

3. To serve, pour the boiling water over the contents of the jar. Seal tightly and shake gently a few times, then leave for 3 minutes, or as long as the packet says it will take for the noodles to become tender. Carefully loosen the lid (which may be hot), then season the broth with a little of the sauce, and eat straight away, adding more sauce as you work your way down the jar.

Mussels
with 'Nduja & Cavolo Nero

Sweet mussels, creamy beans and the sour-hot pop of 'nduja. Clean the mussels well in cold water, pulling off the 'beards' and scraping off any barnacles. Discard any open shells if they don't close when tapped (they are not safe to eat), and also discard those with broken shells.

PREP TIME 30 MINUTES • **COOK TIME 15 MINUTES**

SoF / NF • **SERVES 4**

- 200g (7oz) cavolo nero, ribs removed, leaves finely sliced
- a generous knob of butter
- 1 onion, finely chopped
- 1 small head of fennel, finely sliced, fronds reserved
- 1 handful flat leaf parsley, leaves and stalks separated, both finely chopped
- 3 cloves of garlic, finely sliced
- 100g (3½oz) 'nduja, crumbled
- 200ml (7fl oz) dry white wine
- 1 × 400g (14oz) can cannellini beans in water, drained and rinsed
- 1.75–2kg (3lb 13oz–4lb 8oz) fresh mussels, cleaned (see introduction above)
- zest and juice of ½ unwaxed lemon (see Tip, page 82)
- 1 red chilli, finely chopped
- salt and freshly ground black pepper
- buttered bread (optional, WF / GF if needed, lightly toasted if liked), to serve

1. Steam the cavolo nero with a little water and a pinch of salt until tender, either in a covered pan over a low–medium heat for about 5 minutes, or in a covered bowl in the microwave for 3 minutes. Set aside.

2. Place a large pan over a medium heat and add the butter. When foaming, add the onion, fennel and parsley stalks, and sauté for about 5 minutes, or until the onion is translucent. Add the garlic and 'nduja and cook, stirring, until the 'nduja falls apart. Now add the wine and bring to the boil. Add the drained, steamed kale and the drained beans, stir, turn the heat to high and bring back to a simmer, then add the mussels and clamp on the lid. Cook, shaking the pan every minute or so, until all the mussels have popped open, about 4–5 minutes.

3. Remove the pan from the heat. Squeeze a little lemon juice over the mussels and add the lemon zest, parsley leaves and chilli. Stir once, really gently so that the mussels don't fall out of the shells, then serve in wide bowls, garnished with the reserved fennel fronds. Serve with buttered bread, if liked, to mop up the spicy, bright red broth.

Sea Bream Ceviche

Astoundingly flavourful for something so easy to prepare, ceviche is a quick-marinated raw fish dish from Peru (so the fish must be flappingly fresh and ideally 'sushi grade' – ask your fishmonger).

PREP TIME 15 MINUTES + MARINATING • COOK TIME 0 MINUTES

SoF / NF / WF / GF / DF • SERVES 4 AS A STARTER,

OR AS A MAIN WITH OTHER DISHES

- juice of 3 limes
- juice of ½ orange
- 5mm piece of ginger, peeled and cut into slivers
- 1 garlic clove (omit if using homemade chilli paste or homemade chilli sauce that already contains garlic)
- ½ small red onion or shallot, sliced
- 2 teaspoons Sambal Oelek (see page 188), or 1–2 red chillies, finely chopped, then pummelled to a paste with a pestle and mortar
- scant ½ teaspoon fine salt
- 2 sushi-grade white fish fillets (we like bream or bass), straight from the fridge, and cut into 1–2cm (½–¾in) chunks

TO SERVE:
- coriander leaves
- finely chopped red chilli

1. Place the lime juice, orange juice, ginger and garlic (if using) in a small bowl and set aside.
2. Place the onion in a bowl of iced water and set aside.
3. Once the juices have had about 5 minutes together, add the chilli paste and salt, and mix until the salt has dissolved. Sieve this mixture into a bowl big enough to take the fish, pressing it through to get every bit of flavour out. Taste; it should be sour, slightly sweet and warmingly hot (if you want it hotter, add more chilli paste and strain again). Add the fish and marinate for 10–15 minutes. (Some chefs like to marinate fish for up to 4 hours, but this makes the flesh very firm, so we prefer a shorter time.)
4. Divide the fish between four small plates (reserving the marinade). Drain the onion and arrange a few slices of it on top of each portion, then add a few coriander leaves and a pinch of finely chopped red chilli.
5. The remaining marinade, aka tiger's milk, can be served chilled as a shot (it's purported to be full of health benefits, as well as being a hangover cure), or used in cocktails. (Mixed with the Peruvian spirit pisco, it becomes panther's milk.) Keep chilled and use within 24 hours.

Smoked Paprika Baked Fish
with Fennel & Beans

One pan, heaps of flavour.

PREP TIME 15 MINUTES • COOK TIME 35 MINUTES + RESTING

SoF / NF / WF / GF / DF • SERVES 2

- ½ head of fennel, cored, fronds reserved for garnish
- 1 small onion or 3 shallots
- 6 cherry tomatoes, halved horizontally
- 2 tablespoons olive oil
- 1 × 400g (14oz) can cannellini beans in water, drained and rinsed
- ½ teaspoon sweet smoked paprika
- a pinch of red chilli flakes
- 2 white fish fillets (haddock, cod or hake all work well)
- zest and juice of ½ unwaxed lemon (see Tip, page 82)
- 1 tablespoon chopped flat leaf parsley leaves
- salt and freshly ground black pepper

1. Heat the oven to 200°C/425°F/gas mark 7.
2. Cut the fennel and onion into slices about 7cm (2¾in) thick, then place in a large baking dish with the tomatoes. Drizzle over the olive oil and toss so that everything is lightly coated. Roast for 20 minutes.
3. Add the beans, smoked paprika, a good pinch of salt, some black pepper and the red chilli flakes. Toss everything again – don't worry if the tomatoes start to fall apart. Pat the fish dry, then gently place in the dish and turn a couple of times to lightly coat in the smoky oil. Season, then rest the fish on top of the vegetables, and return the dish to the oven for 15 minutes.
4. When the fish is done, it should be just flaking apart. Set the dish aside to rest for 5 minutes. Before serving, squeeze over the lemon juice and sprinkle with the lemon zest, the fennel fronds (chopped, if large) and the parsley.

Harissa Salmon

You know those days when you crave a meal that feels incredibly wholesome,
but also tastes fabulous? This is for those days.

PREP TIME 15 MINUTES + MARINATING • COOK TIME 30 MINUTES

SoF / NF / WF / GF / DF • SERVES 4

- 4 skin-on trout or salmon fillets (sustainably sourced)
- 3 heaped tablespoons harissa paste
- 3 tablespoons olive oil, plus an extra splash for the veg
- 1 tablespoon freshly squeezed lemon juice, plus extra for the veg
- ¼ teaspoon ground cumin
- 250g (9oz) brown rice
- 100g (3½oz) fine green beans, trimmed and halved if long
- 8 asparagus spears, halved lengthways and sliced into 4–5cm (1½–2in) pieces
- 100g (3½oz) Tenderstem or purple sprouting broccoli, each floret halved lengthways
- 100g (3½oz) cucumber, finely sliced
- 100g (3½oz) radishes, finely sliced
- salt and freshly ground black pepper

1. Place the fish on a plate, skin-side down, and season it lightly. Combine the harissa, olive oil, measured lemon juice, cumin and some black black pepper in a bowl, then spoon the mixture over the fish. Set aside to marinate for about 30 minutes.

2. Meanwhile, cook the rice: place it in a saucepan with a pinch of salt and pour in enough boiling water to cover it by 1.5cm (⅝in). Bring to a simmer, then cover and cook for about 30 minutes, until it is tender and has absorbed all the water. Fluff up with a fork, cover again and set aside until needed.

3. Heat the oven to 200°C/425°F/gas mark 7. Line a baking tray with nonstick baking paper.

4. Place the fish in the prepared tray, skin-side down, and scrape in all the remaining marinade. Bake for 10 minutes.

5. Meanwhile, blanch the beans, asparagus and broccoli in a pan with a pinch of salt and about 5cm (2in) boiling water for 2 minutes. Drain, return to the pan and add a splash of olive oil, a dash of lemon juice and another pinch of salt. Toss together.

6. Place the cucumber and radishes in a small bowl and stir in a squeeze of lemon juice and a pinch of salt.

7. Divide the rice between four bowls, then add the vegetables. Peel the skin off the fish, then roughly flake the flesh and arrange over the veg. Drizzle with the remaining marinade, and finally sprinkle with the cucumber and radishes.

Baked Mackerel
with Fennel & Apple Pickle

Oily fish pairs really well with a lip-smacking, fresh vegetable and citrus zest pickle.

PREP TIME 20 MINUTES • COOK TIME 20 MINUTES

SoF / NF / WF / GF • SERVES 4

- 4 mackerel, cleaned and gutted, heads and tails left on
- 12 bay leaves
- 12 thin half-moon lemon slices
- 4 knobs of butter
- salt and freshly ground black pepper

FOR THE PICKLE:
- 100ml (3½fl oz) cider vinegar
- 2 tablespoons caster sugar
- 1 teaspoon fine salt
- pared zest of ½ unwaxed orange (see Tip, page 82), cut into fine slices
- 8 black peppercorns
- 1 bay leaf
- ¼ head of fennel, very finely sliced, fronds reserved
- ½ small onion or 1–2 shallots, very finely sliced
- 1 green apple, very finely sliced
- 1 small carrot, very finely sliced
- 50g (1¾oz) cucumber, very finely sliced

1. Heat the oven to 200°C/425°F/gas mark 7. Line a large roasting tray with baking paper.
2. Pat the fish dry with kitchen paper, then sit them on top of the baking paper. Season all over. Tuck 3 bay leaves into the cavity of each fish, along with 3 slices of lemon. Dot the top of each fish with butter and put a small piece in the cavity too. Transfer the tray to the oven and bake for 20 minutes, basting once with the pan juices halfway through. Set aside for 5 minutes.
3. While the fish cook, make the pickle: place the cider vinegar, sugar, salt, orange zest, peppercorns and bay leaf in a small pan and bring to a simmer, stirring occasionally to help the sugar and salt dissolve. Put the finely sliced vegetables in a large bowl and pour in the vinegar mixture. Stir well and set aside.
4. When ready to serve, place the fish on warmed plates. Drain a portion of the pickle and place it alongside the fish. Garnish with the reserved fennel fronds.

TIP

A mandoline is very handy for making dishes that require finely sliced ingredients. To prevent grated fingers, you can wear a protective mesh glove (available online).

Burrata
with Wilted Greens

This is inspired by a dish on the menu at a lovely Italian restaurant called Trullo, which thoroughly brightened up a wet, cold spring day in north London.

PREP TIME 10 MINUTES

SoF / NF / WF / GF / V

COOK TIME 5 MINUTES

SERVES 4 AS A STARTER,

OR 2 AS A MAIN WITH OTHER DISHES

- 75g (2¾oz) baby spinach
- 75g (2¾oz) rocket
- zest and juice of 1 unwaxed lemon (see Tip, page 82)
- extra-virgin olive oil
- 1 large ball (250g/9oz) of burrata, at room temperature
- flaky sea salt

1. Place the wet spinach and rocket in a pan over a medium heat with a splash of water. Cover and steam until wilted, 3–4 minutes. Drain well, using the back of a spoon to press out as much liquid as possible. Return the greens to the pan and add a pinch of salt, a squeeze of lemon juice and a splash of olive oil. Toss, then set aside until warm rather than hot.

2. Place the burrata on a serving dish and gently slice across the top so the creamy centre opens out a little, but don't cut all the way through. Strew the top and sides of the cheese with the wilted greens, then spoon over about 1 tablespoon olive oil and another squeeze of lemon juice. Sprinkle with the lemon zest and a pinch of salt, then serve straight away.

TIP

Get the wobbly burrata out of the fridge and drain off its liquid an hour or two before you want to serve it.

Miso Aubergine

Here is our take on a Japanese dish called nasu dengaku. The way the aubergine is cut allows the sweet miso to sink into the flesh, then char slightly as it grills. This produces a lovely smoky flavour, against a salty-sweet backdrop.

PREP TIME 15 MINUTES • **COOK TIME 22 MINUTES**
NF / WF / GF / DF / V / Ve • **SERVES 2**

- 1 slender aubergine (this will cook faster than a bulbous one)
- 3–4 tablespoons neutral oil, for cooking
- 2 tablespoons miso paste (WF / GF if needed)
- 1 tablespoon maple syrup (or honey if not Ve)
- ½ teaspoon white wine vinegar
- 1 teaspoon toasted sesame oil
- 1 tablespoon hot water

TO SERVE:
- sesame seeds
- finely sliced spring onion
- freshly cooked rice (ideally, Japanese short-grain)

1. Use an ovenproof frying pan for this, if you have one (just to save on washing up). Halve the aubergine lengthways, then use a sharp knife to score a criss-cross pattern into the flesh without cutting through the skin.

2. Pour the oil into a frying pan set over a medium heat and, when hot, add the aubergine halves, cut-side down. Cook for 6–8 minutes, until deep golden brown, checking to ensure the flesh isn't burning. Turn and cook until the skin starts to wrinkle and you can see that the flesh inside is softening.

3. Stir together the miso paste, honey, vinegar, sesame oil and hot water.

4. Heat the grill to its highest setting.

5. Divide the miso mixture between the two halves of aubergine, spooning and spreading it evenly over the cut sides. Place the pan under the hot grill, about 10cm (4in) below the heat source, and cook for about 5 minutes, keeping a close eye as miso burns easily.

6. Once the miso is bubbling and the aubergine is just beginning to char, transfer to two serving plates. Sprinkle each half with the sesame seeds and spring onions, and serve with freshly cooked rice on the side.

TIP

Steamed pak choi dressed in garlic and ginger is a lovely side to this, or try some good quality ready-made pot-sticker dumplings or gyoza.

Ricotta Balls in Arrabiata Sauce

Delicious as a light meal on their own, or with some freshly cooked pasta or a hunk of warm focaccia.

PREP TIME 20 MINUTES • COOK TIME 50 MINUTES

SoF / NF / V • SERVES 4

- 250g (9oz) ricotta cheese
- 2 tablespoons breadcrumbs, plus extra for crumbing
- 3 tablespoons plain flour
- ½ teaspoon baking powder
- 3 eggs, beaten
- freshly grated nutmeg
- a pinch of white pepper
- 4 tablespoons freshly grated Parmesan cheese, plus extra to serve (check V, if needed)
- zest of ½ unwaxed lemon (see Tip, page 82)
- 3 tablespoons very finely chopped flat leaf parsley
- 2 cloves of garlic, crushed
- olive oil, for cooking

FOR THE ARRABIATA SAUCE:
- extra-virgin olive oil
- 3 cloves of garlic, finely chopped
- 2 red chillies, very finely chopped
- 2 × 400g (14oz) cans finely chopped tomatoes (we like Mutti Polpa for this), or 700ml (1¼ pints) tomato passata
- a pinch of chilli flakes, or more to taste (the sauce should be fiery)
- salt and freshly ground black pepper
- leaves from a small bunch of basil

1. First make the sauce. Place a heavy-based pan over a medium heat, add a tablespoonful of olive oil and cook the garlic and chopped chillies, stirring constantly, for 30–60 seconds without browning. Stir in the tomatoes and bring to a simmer. Add the chilli flakes and a pinch of salt, then partly cover with a lid and leave to cook very gently, stirring every 10 minutes or so, for at least 30 minutes. If it reduces too quickly and becomes sticky, turn the heat down and add a splash of water – the aim is for the tomatoes to break down and release their sweetness without thickening too much.

2. Meanwhile, place the ricotta in a bowl with the measured breadcrumbs, flour, baking powder, 1 beaten egg, a dusting of nutmeg, the white pepper, Parmesan, lemon zest, parsley, garlic and 1 tablespoon of olive oil, and mix together thoroughly. Chill for 20 minutes to firm up.

3. Heat the oven to 180°C/400°F/gas mark 6. Line a baking tray with nonstick baking paper and brush it with olive oil.

4. Half-fill a small bowl with the extra breadcrumbs, add 1 tablespoon olive oil and toss well. Place the remaining beaten eggs in another small bowl.

5. Shape the chilled ricotta mixture into 16 equal balls. Dip each in the beaten egg, allow the excess to drain off, then dip in the breadcrumbs. Place on the tray and bake for 20 minutes.

6. When ready to serve, taste the sauce: it should be rich with chilli heat, and tart and sweet from the tomatoes. Tear up half the basil leaves and stir them into the sauce.

7. Serve the ricotta balls on top of the sauce, with more fresh basil leaves and a generous grating of fresh Parmesan.

Baked Leeks
with Cheese & Hazelnuts

Creamy, comforting and sweet baked leeks with a crunchy cheesy topping. If you're not a fan of blue cheese, this works just as well without it – simply add a little Parmesan instead.

PREP TIME 15 MINUTES • COOK TIME 38 MINUTES

SoF / V • SERVES 2 AS A MAIN, OR 4 AS A SIDE

- 5 leeks, white parts only
- a knob of butter, plus extra for greasing
- 1 heaped tablespoon plain flour
- 175ml (6fl oz) milk
- 100ml (3½fl oz) double cream
- a pinch of freshly grated nutmeg
- 2 teaspoons fresh thyme leaves (optional)
- 100g (3½oz) blue cheese, crumbled into chunks (optional), or freshly grated Parmesan cheese (check V, if needed)
- 2 tablespoons crispy onions, from a packet (or you can caramelize 1 finely sliced onion in a little butter)
- ½ ball (about 75g/2¾oz) mozzarella cheese, torn into pieces
- 3 tablespoons chopped blanched hazelnuts
- salt and freshly ground black pepper

TO SERVE:
- green salad
- buttered crusty bread

1. Halve the leeks lengthways and discard the outer two or three layers, as they will be tough and chewy if left in the final dish. Cut what remains into 4cm (1½in) chunks, keeping their semicircular shape intact, if you can. Wash gently, rinsing away any grit trapped between the layers.

2. Place the leeks in a heatproof bowl with a splash of water. Cover and steam for 4 minutes in the microwave, then allow to stand for 2 minutes. Alternatively, place in a steamer basket set over a pan of simmering water for 8 minutes.

3. While the leeks cook, place the butter in a saucepan over a medium heat. When melted and bubbling, add the flour, and cook, stirring, for a couple of minutes, until it forms a golden paste. Turn the heat to low and gradually add the milk a little at a time, stirring constantly, until you have a smooth sauce. Remove from the heat and add the cream, nutmeg, thyme, if using, salt and pepper. If you're not using the blue cheese in the next step, add 2 tablespoons of freshly grated Parmesan to the sauce now.

4. Butter a medium-sized baking dish and arrange the steamed leeks in it in a single layer, tucking the blue cheese, if using, in between. Sprinkle over the crispy onions, then pour the sauce over the leeks. Dot with the mozzarella, then grate a thin layer of Parmesan over the top. Bake for 15 minutes.

5. Sprinkle over the hazelnuts, then return to the oven for 15 minutes, until the cheese is bubbling and the nuts toasted. Eat with the green salad and crusty hunk of buttered bread.

Avocado Mojo Verde Potatoes
with Fried Eggs

Mojo verde is a green sauce from the Canary Islands, where it's traditionally served with potatoes cooked in really salty water (at one time, seawater). We often make the sauce with avocado for creaminess, but without chilli to let the other flavours really sing.

PREP TIME 15 MINUTESG • COOK TIME 40 MINUTES

SoF / NF / WF / GF / DF / V • SERVES 4

- about 900g (2lb) small, waxy potatoes, halved and unpeeled
- 3 tablespoons flaky sea salt
- olive oil, for cooking
- 1–2 eggs per person

FOR THE MOJO VERDE:

- 50g (1¾oz) (a very large bunch) coriander, leaves only, finely chopped
- 4 cloves of garlic, roughly chopped
- 1 sweet green pepper, roughly chopped
- 1 green chilli, roughly chopped (optional)
- 6 tablespoons olive oil (nothing too peppery)
- 2 tablespoons sherry vinegar
- 1 teaspoon ground cumin
- 1 avocado
- 1 teaspoon flaky salt

1. Place the potatoes in a large pan in a single layer. Add the salt, then pour in enough boiling water to almost but not quite cover the potatoes. Place over a medium–high heat and bring back to the boil. Simmer for 30 minutes, uncovered, turning each potato once after 20 minutes. The water will reduce during cooking.

2. Meanwhile, place all the mojo ingredients in blender or small food processor, and blitz to form a rough but saucy purée. Set aside.

3. When the potatoes are cooked, drain and return them to the pan – they will look dusty with the remnants of the salt. Shake them gently a couple of times to wrinkle the skins, but not so much that they break up. Set aside.

4. Place a large frying pan over a high heat. Add a splash of olive oil, then fry the eggs until done to your liking.

5. Roughly chop the potatoes, spoon over some of the sauce, reserving the rest to serve, then toss to coat. Divide between four plates, then top with the fried eggs and more sauce.

Crispy Baked Tofu

Rebecca's friend Tiff gave her this recipe, and it's better-tasting than many (highly processed) meat alternatives. Use it instead of pulled meat of any kind – in curries, in brioche buns, tacos or burritos, or even dressed with herby mayo in a sandwich.

PREP TIME 10 MINUTES • COOK TIME 30 MINUTES

NF / WF / GF / DF / V / Ve • SERVES 4

- 1 × 450g (1lb) block of extra-firm tofu
- 1 tablespoon soy sauce (WF / GF if needed)
- ½ teaspoon garlic powder
- 1 tablespoon neutral oil

1. Heat the oven to 180°C/400°F/gas mark 6. Line a large baking tray (or two smaller ones) with nonstick baking paper and brush with oil.
2. Cut the tofu block into quarters, then grate it coarsely. Place in a bowl, add the soy sauce, garlic powder and oil and toss gently but thoroughly.
3. Tip the tofu onto the baking tray and spread out in a thin layer – it will look like a lot, but will shrink during cooking. Bake for 25–30 minutes, shimmying it about and turning it once with a spatula halfway through, depending on whether you want it tender or crisp.

TIP

Depending on how you plan to use this, you can add other flavours, such as sweet or smoked paprika, sesame oil, ground cumin or coriander, curry powder, Chinese five-spice, ras el hanout or berbere spice blend.

5

FULL-ON FEASTS

Loaded LEON Fries
with Spiced Lamb Kofta

All the best flavours from a late-night kebab pitstop, but made with good-quality lamb and eaten in the comfort of your own home – what's not to like? We love the way our LEON waffle fries absorb the kofta juices while cooking, but ready-made sweet potato fries or homemade wedges also work well. (You will find our criss-cross cut waffle fries in the freezer aisle of several major supermarkets, or we've given a recipe to make your own sweet potato wedges below).

PREP TIME 20 MINUTES • COOK TIME 25–35 MINUTES

SoF / NF / WF / GF • SERVES 4

- 1 × 550g (1lb 4oz) bag of LEON waffle fries or sweet potato fries (or see below for homemade sweet potato wedges)

FOR THE SWEET POTATO WEDGES (IF MAKING):
- 1kg (2lb 4oz) sweet potatoes
- 4 tablespoons olive oil
- 2 tablespoons smoked paprika
- 2 tabslespoons garlic powder
- 2 tablespoons polenta
- 1 teaspoon fine salt

FOR THE KOFTA:
- 500g (1lb 2oz) good-quality minced lamb (at least 20% fat)
- ½ red onion, grated
- 1 clove of garlic, grated
- a generous pinch of chilli flakes
- 1 teaspoon ground cumin
- ¼ teaspoon ground cinnamon
- 1 teaspoon paprika
- 4 tablespoons dried breadcrumbs (WF / GF if needed)
- 4 tablespoons milk

1. Heat the oven to 200°C/425°F/gas mark 7.

2. If making your own sweet potato wedges, make them first. Scrub the sweet potatoes but leave the skin on, then cut into wedges, about 2cm (¾in) thick. Put the wedges on a large rimmed baking tray with the olive oil, smoked paprika, garlic powder, polenta and fine salt. Using your hands, mix together to thoroughly coat the wedges. Put the baking tray in the hot oven to bake for 20 minutes.

3. If using ready-made LEON waffle fries or sweet potato fries, these need a little less cooking time, so arrange the fries in a single layer on a large rimmed baking tray and put in the hot oven to bake for 10 minutes.

4. While you wait for the sweet potato wedges or waffle fries to cook, make the kofta. Place all the kofta ingredients in a bowl and mix together with your hands. Divide the mixture into 12 equal pieces and shape into fat little oblongs. Set aside.

5. After the fries have had 10 minutes baking time (or the homemade wedges have had 20 minutes baking time), arrange the kofta on top of and alongside the fries or

Continued overleaf ⟶

- 2 tablespoons very finely chopped fresh flat leaf parsley
- 2 tablespoons very finely chopped fresh mint
- 1 teaspoon fresh thyme leaves
- ¾ teaspoon fine salt and lots of freshly ground black pepper

FOR THE HOT TOMATO SAUCE:
- 2 tablespoons extra hot sauce (we use Encona)
- 2 tablespoons tomato ketchup

FOR THE GARLIC SAUCE:
- 2 tablespoons Greek-style yoghurt
- 2 tablespoons mayonnaise
- 2 teaspoons lemon juice
- 1 clove of garlic, crushed to a paste

FOR THE GARNISH:
- 1 small shallot, finely sliced
- 6 radishes, finely sliced
- 8cm (3¼in) piece of cucumber, cut into matchsticks
- ¼ small head of fennel, finely sliced
- 1 tablespoon freshly squeezed lemon juice
- a generous pinch of sumac
- 2 long pickled chillies, sliced
- a handful of flat leaf parsley leaves, roughly chopped

wedges, then return the full baking tray to the oven for 15 minutes more.

6. Meanwhile, make the sauces. Stir the hot sauce and ketchup together in one bowl. In another bowl, stir together the yoghurt, mayo, lemon juice, garlic and a pinch of salt. Set aside.

7. Now prepare the garnish. Place the shallot, radish, cucumber and fennel in a bowl. Squeeze over the lemon juice and add a pinch of salt and a generous pinch of sumac. Stir and set aside.

8. At the end of the cooking time, the fries should be golden and the kofta just cooked through. Scatter the sumac vegetables, pickled chillies and chopped parsley over the tray. Spoon some of each sauce over the top. To serve, place the tray in the middle of the table, with the remaining sauces alongside.

TIP

Vegetarians can swap the kofta for crumbled feta and purple olives added alongside the sumac vegetables.

LEON Makhani Squash Curry

In order to be allergy friendly, and because we love the taste, we make our rich makhani curry with coconut milk instead of the traditional cream. We serve it with brown rice, both for its flavour and for its high fibre and wide range of nutrients. You might be most familiar with dal makhani, which is made with lentils, but you can also make paneer makhani or chicken makhani – despite being quite different dishes, a distinctive creamy, butteriness is what they all have in common (makhani is a Punjabi word meaning butter, or buttery). Feel free to experiment with other cooked pulses or different vegetables here; just reduce the cooking time if you want to use something like courgette or aubergine.

PREP TIME 20 MINUTES • COOK TIME 50 MINUTES

SoF / NF / WF / GF / V • SERVES 4

- 1 butternut squash, peeled, deseeded and cut into large chunks
- rapeseed or olive oil, for cooking
- 250g (9oz) brown rice, rinsed
- 1 teaspoon sunflower seeds
- 1 teaspoon linseeds
- 1 teaspoon pumpkin seeds
- salt and freshly ground black pepper

FOR THE MAKHANI:
- rapeseed or olive oil, for cooking
- ½ onion, finely chopped
- 2 cloves of garlic, crushed or finely grated
- 3cm (1¼in) piece of ginger, peeled and finely grated
- ½ teaspoon ground green cardamom (seeds from 10–12 pods, see Tip overleaf)
- 2 teaspoons ground black cardamom (seeds from 4 pods, see Tip overleaf)
- ½ teaspoon ground cloves
- 1 bay leaf
- 1 teaspoon ground turmeric
- 2 teaspoons Kashmiri chilli powder (or see Tip overleaf)

1. Heat the oven to 200°C/425°F/gas mark 7. Place the squash in a roasting tray, drizzle with olive oil and toss to coat. Roast for 30 minutes.

2. Meanwhile, add the brown rice and a pinch of salt to a large pan. Cover with 500ml (18fl oz) freshly boiled water and bring to a simmer over a medium heat. Cover and cook until the rice is tender, 25–35 minutes, topping up with a splash of water if it looks as though it will boil dry well before it's ready. When cooked, fluff up with a fork, then cover and set aside.

3. Once the squash is tender and lightly charred, set aside.

4. While the rice and squash are cooking, start the makhani: place a large, wide pan over a medium heat and add a splash of cooking oil. When hot, add the onion and a pinch of salt and sauté for 5–6 minutes, until just turning translucent. Add the garlic and ginger and fry for a further 2 minutes. Turn the heat to low and add the green and black cardamom, the cloves, bay leaf, turmeric and chilli powder and continue to fry for 3 minutes, stirring often and being careful not to let the spices burn.

Continued overleaf →

- 1 × 400g (14oz) can of chopped tomatoes
- 200ml (7fl oz) coconut milk
- 30g (1oz) butter (or DF or Ve alternative, if needed)
- 1 teaspoon garam masala
- 1 teaspoon dark brown sugar
- 1 tablespoon dried fenugreek leaves
- 1 × 400g (14oz) can chickpeas in water, drained and rinsed

TO SERVE:
- 5–6 tablespoons plain yoghurt (DF or Ve if needed, coconut yoghurt is good here)
- a handful of coriander leaves
- a handful of mint leaves

5. Add the tomatoes and bring to a simmer. Partly cover with a lid, and allow to cook for 30 minutes, until the oil rises to the top of the curry, stirring every now and then to prevent sticking. Stir in the coconut milk, butter, garam masala, sugar and fenugreek and simmer for 10 minutes. Remove from the heat and use a blender to blitz the sauce until smooth.

6. Add the chickpeas and roasted squash to the sauce, then reheat to warm through. Taste and season generously with salt and freshly ground black pepper.

7. Meanwhile, lightly toast the seeds in a hot, dry pan for just a minute or two.

8. Divide the brown rice between four shallow bowls, and spoon over the curry. Add a dollop of the yoghurt to the side of each bowl. Sprinkle each serving with the herbs and toasted seeds.

TIP

If you don't have Kashmiri chilli powder, which is bright red but mild, mix 2 teaspoons of paprika with ½ teaspoon of regular chilli powder. Black cardamoms are bigger than green ones, and are dried over an open fire, so have a wonderfully smoky aroma. It's often easier to find both black and green cardamoms as whole spices in the World Foods aisle of a supermarket, in which case you will need to break open the pods and grind up the seeds using a pestle and mortar.

Chantal's Plantain Curry

This sour yet creamy vegan curry – which has quite a kick – occasionally has a special guest role on our restaurant menus. It was originally created by LEON's former development chef Chantal Symons.

PREP TIME 20 MINUTES • COOK TIME 1¾ HOURS

SoF / NF / WF / GF / DF / V / Ve • SERVES 4–6

- 2 tablespoons coconut oil, for cooking
- 2 onions, diced
- 1 head of garlic, peeled and finely chopped
- 1½ tablespoons finely chopped fresh thyme
- 2 tablespoons mild curry powder
- ½ teaspoon ground allspice
- 1 × 400ml (14fl oz) can full-fat coconut milk
- 800ml (28fl oz) water
- 1 large carrot, quartered lengthways and diced
- 3 plantains, sliced on an angle into 1cm (½in) pieces
- 1 Scotch bonnet chilli, left whole
- 1 bay leaf
- 1 tablespoon vegan bouillon powder (WF if needed)
- 250g (9oz) spring greens, ribs removed, leaves sliced into 1cm (½in) ribbons
- zest and juice of 1 lime
- 2 tablespoons chopped coriander leaves
- 1 teaspoon salt
- freshly ground black pepper

FOR THE COCONUT RICE:
- 250g (9oz) basmati rice, rinsed
- 250ml (9fl oz) water
- 250ml (9fl oz) coconut milk
- ¼ teaspoon fine salt

1. Place a large pan over a medium heat. Add the oil and onions, and sweat for 5 minutes. Add the garlic and thyme and cook for another 10 minutes. Stir in the spices and a twist of black pepper, then add the salt, coconut milk, water, carrot, plantains, chilli, bay leaf and bouillon. Simmer for 45–60 minutes, or until the plantain is tender and the sauce has reduced and thickened. Add the spring greens, then cover and cook for another 10 minutes.

2. About 30 minutes before the curry is ready, place the rinsed rice, water, coconut milk and salt in a saucepan. Set over a medium heat and bring to the boil, then cover with a lid and simmer for 12 minutes. Remove from the heat, fluff up with a fork, cover again and leave to stand until needed.

3. Just before serving, fish out and discard the chilli (it might have disintegrated, which is fine – you just wouldn't want to accidentally eat it whole). Add the lime zest and juice, stir through the coriander leaves, then serve with the coconut rice.

Devilled Paneer & Chickpeas

Creamy paneer is a perfect match for this sharp, hot curry.

PREP TIME 15 MINUTES • COOK TIME 20 MINUTES

NF / WF / GF / V • SERVES 2 AS A MAIN, OR 4 WITH OTHER DISHES

- 225–250g (8–9oz) paneer, depending on pack size
- ½ teaspoon ground turmeric
- 2 teaspoons soy sauce (WF / GF if needed)
- neutral oil, for cooking
- 4 cloves of garlic, crushed
- 4cm (1½in) piece of ginger, peeled and finely grated
- 1 red chilli, finely chopped
- ¼ teaspoon chilli powder
- 4 tablespoons tomato ketchup
- 1 teaspoon cider vinegar
- 150ml (5fl oz) hot water
- ½ onion, finely sliced
- 1 red pepper, finely sliced
- 1 fresh tomato, deseeded and chopped
- 125g (4½oz) cooked chickpeas from a can or jar
- fine salt
- steamed rice, to serve (60–75g/2¼–2¾oz uncooked rice per person)

1. Pat the paneer dry with kitchen paper and cut into 2cm (¾in) cubes (don't worry if it crumbles). Place in a bowl with a pinch of salt, the turmeric and 1 teaspoon of the soy sauce. Gently toss to coat, then set aside.

2. Place a wide pan over a medium heat and add a splash of oil. Once hot, add the garlic, ginger and chopped chilli (all at the same time) and cook, stirring constantly, for just 1 minute. Immediately add the chilli powder, ketchup, remaining teaspoon of soy sauce and the vinegar, stir a couple of times, then add the water. Bring up to a simmer.

3. Place another splash of oil in a separate frying pan over a high heat and fry the onion and red pepper for 5 minutes. Tip into the wide pan, along with the tomato. Add a little more oil to the pan, then use tongs to place the paneer in it and cook, turning, until crisp and golden all over, 2–3 minutes a side.

4. Add the chickpeas to the pan. If the sauce is still quite liquid, turn the heat up to reduce it. Taste – it should be sour, sharp and spicy; add more salt or chilli powder, as needed.

5. Just before serving, tip the crisp paneer into the sauce and toss together. Serve with the steamed rice.

TIP

If you want to make this into a main course for 4 people without needing any other dishes, just double each ingredient listed above.

Green Curry

Look out for our green curry, a long-term favourite that is often on the menu.
We currently do one with chicken, baby sweetcorn, carrots and edamame beans.

PREP TIME 20–25 MINUTES • COOK TIME UP TO 35 MINUTES

NF / WF / GF / DF • SERVES 4

- 2 × 400ml (14fl oz) cans full-fat coconut milk
- 250ml (9fl oz) hot chicken stock
- 8 lime leaves
- 300g (10½oz) vegetables (Thai aubergines, sweet potato, squash, baby corn, long green beans, bamboo shoots, peppers, carrots, edamame or mangetout) cut into bite-sized pieces
- 650g (1lb 7oz) skinless, boneless chicken thighs (or steak, fish, seafood, fried tofu), cut into bite-sized pieces or strips
- leaves from 2 sprigs of Thai basil
- 1 red chilli, thinly sliced on an angle
- fish sauce, to season
- freshly ground black pepper
- freshly cooked jasmine rice (allow 60–75g/2¼–2¾oz uncooked rice per person), to serve

1. Start by making the paste: put all the ingredients into a blender and blitz until you have a smooth, slightly glossy-looking paste. (This can also be done using a stick blender or mortar and pestle.)

2. Open one can of coconut milk without shaking it and scoop a tablespoon of the thick cream from the top into a large, deep pan. Place over a medium heat until the cream sizzles and splits. Quickly add the paste and fry, stirring often, for 5 minutes, or until the bright green oil is released and the paste thickens rather than looking wet. Once it smells fragrant but no longer raw, add the remaining coconut milk, stock and lime leaves and gently bring to a simmer.

3. If adding vegetables, such as sweet potato and squash, that need more cooking than the chicken or other chosen protein, add them now and cook until just tender, before adding the protein. Chicken pieces will need about 10 minutes, but salmon, tofu and crisp vegetables, such as green beans, will need only a few minutes in the broth. If you find there isn't enough liquid to cover everything in the pan, add a little hot water and bring back to a simmer.

4. Once everything is cooked, remove from the heat and add half the Thai basil leaves and sliced red chillies. Taste the broth and add some fish sauce or salt, as needed. Serve with jasmine rice and garnish each bowlful with the remaining Thai basil and red chillies.

TIP

You can make this vegan by swapping out the protein for a vegan option, using vegetable stock and replacing the fish sauce with either salt or seaweed powder, to taste.

FOR THE PASTE:

- 5 green chillies, very finely chopped
- 3 shallots, very finely chopped
- 5 cloves of garlic, crushed
- 2 teaspoons galangal paste, from a jar
- 1 stick of lemongrass, tough outer skin discarded, very finely chopped
- zest of ½ unwaxed lime, preferably makrut lime (see Tip, page 82)
- 1 teaspoon ground coriander
- ½ teaspoon ground cumin
- ½ teaspoon ground turmeric
- 3 tablespoons very finely chopped coriander stalks or root
- 1 teaspoon fish sauce or Thai shrimp paste

Karaage Chicken Rice Bowl
with Sweet Soy Sauce

We tried a dish like this in our favourite noodle bar, Koya, in Soho, and the ridiculously crisp batter and juicy marinated chicken inside meant we immediately decided we needed an at-home version. Don't be scared of deep-frying the eggs – they don't explode, but instead puff up in a fun and very satisfying way.

PREP TIME 25 MINUTES + 30 MINUTES MARINATING • COOK TIME 45 MINUTES

NF / WF / GF / DF • SERVES 4

- 4 skinless, boneless chicken thigh fillets
- 2 tablespoons mirin (sweet rice wine)
- 1 tablespoon toasted sesame oil
- 2 cloves of garlic, finely grated
- 3cm (1¼in) piece of ginger, peeled and finely grated
- 2 tablespoons soy sauce (WF / GF if needed)
- 300g (10½oz) Japanese short-grain (sushi) rice
- 450ml (16fl oz) cold water
- neutral oil, for cooking
- 150g (5½oz) potato starch
- 2 tablespoons cornflour
- 4 eggs
- salt and freshly ground black pepper

FOR THE SWEET SOY SAUCE:
- 2 tablespoons mirin
- 4 tablespoons soy sauce (WF / GF if needed)
- 2 tablespoons sugar
- 2 teaspoons rice vinegar (or cider vinegar)
- 2 tablespoons dashi or vegetable stock
- 1 clove of garlic, finely grated or crushed
- 1cm (½in) piece of ginger, peeled and finely grated

1. Cut the chicken thighs into bite-sized pieces and place in a bowl with the mirin, sesame oil, garlic, ginger, soy sauce and some salt and pepper. Stir well to ensure the meat is well coated. Cover and set aside in the fridge for at least 30 minutes.

2. Place the sweet soy sauce ingredients in a small pan over a medium heat. Bring just to boiling, then immediately remove from the heat. Set aside.

3. Stir all the soy mayonnaise ingredients together in a jug.

4. Rinse the rice, then place in a large pan along with a pinch of salt. Add the water, cover with a lid and bring up to a simmer. Turn the heat to medium–low and cook for 20 minutes. Fluff up the rice with a fork, cover again and set aside for 10 minutes, or until needed.

5. Pour about 8cm (3¼in) of cooking oil into a deep saucepan over a medium heat. When it registers about 175°C/345°F on a thermometer, or a cube of bread added to the oil browns in about 30 seconds, it's ready to use. (If it's too hot, lower the heat.)

6. Meanwhile, heat the oven to its lowest setting. Line a large plate with kitchen paper.

7. Put the potato starch and cornflour in a bowl and mix well. Use a slotted spoon to lift the chicken pieces from the

FOR THE MAYONNAISE:
- 3 tablespoons mayonnaise
- 1 teaspoon sesame oil
- 1 teaspoon lime juice
- 1 teaspoon soy sauce (WF / GF if needed)

TO SERVE:
- 2 spring onions, finely sliced on an angle
- 2 heaped tablespoons pickled sushi ginger, drained and finely sliced
- lemon or lime wedges

TIP

Potato starch, which is a very fine flour, is available online or in Japanese supermarkets; if you can't find it, use cornflour instead.

marinade, letting the liquid drain away before dredging them in the flour; shake each piece really well to remove any excess. Place on an unlined plate while you coat the rest.

8. When the oil is ready, cook 3–4 chicken pieces at a time; don't crowd the pan as this will lower the temperature of the oil and make for a soggy result. Fry the chicken for about 5 minutes, turning once halfway through, until crisp, light golden and cooked through. Transfer to the lined plate and keep warm in the oven while cooking the rest.

9. When the chicken is all cooked through, break an egg into a small bowl and gently pour it into the hot oil – it will deep-fry very quickly, puffing up and turning golden. After a minute or less, lift out with a slotted spoon and place on the chicken plate to drain. Repeat with the other three eggs.

10. Serve by dividing the cooked rice between four bowls, then add the fried chicken and one egg per bowl. Top with the spring onions and pickled ginger. Drizzle over a little of the sweet soy sauce, and serve the rest on the table along with the mayo and some lime or lemon wedges.

↬ *Pictured overleaf*

Beef Vindaloo

Dating back 500 years, this curry recipe has to be one of the all-time, most flavourful dishes in food history.

PREP TIME 20 MINUTES + MARINATING   •   COOK TIME 2½ HOURS

SoF / NF / WF / GF /DF   •   SERVES 4

- 800g (1lb 12oz) stewing beef
- 2 tablespoons neutral oil or ghee, for cooking
- 3 onions, finely sliced
- 1 teaspoon mustard seeds
- 2 teaspoons tamarind paste, from a jar

FOR THE MARINADE:
- 5 cloves
- seeds from 6 cardamom pods
- 1 teaspoon fenugreek seeds
- 1 teaspoon coriander seeds
- ½ teaspoon cumin seeds
- ½ teaspoon ground turmeric
- 2 teaspoons paprika (the reddest you can find), or Kashmiri chilli powder
- ½ teaspoon ground cinnamon
- ¼ teaspoon freshly ground black pepper
- ½ teaspoon hot chilli powder
- 2 teaspoons dried red chilli flakes, or more to taste
- 5 cloves of garlic, crushed
- 3cm (1¼in) piece of ginger, peeled and finely grated
- 3 tablespoons red wine vinegar
- generous pinch of salt

TO SERVE:
- steamed rice (allow 60–75g/2¼–2¾oz uncooked rice per person)
- poppadoms and pickles (WF / GF if needed)

1. First make the marinade: grind all the whole spices to a powder using a spice grinder or mortar and pestle. Transfer to a large bowl and mix in the ground spices, chilli powder and chilli flakes, then add the garlic, ginger and vinegar. Mix well, then add the beef and a good pinch of salt. Use your hands to massage the marinade into the meat, then cover and place in the fridge for at least 2 hours, but ideally overnight.

2. When ready to cook, set a large, heavy-based pan over a medium–high heat. Add the oil and the onions, then cook, stirring often, until golden, 10–12 minutes, adding the mustard seeds to the pan for the last couple of minutes. Add the meat and all the marinade and cook for 5 minutes, stirring. Next add 250ml (9fl oz) of hot water. Stir well, scraping up any browned bits from the base of the pan, and bring to a simmer. Turn the heat down, cover and cook for about 2 hours, stirring often and keeping it topped up with water – it shouldn't be wet, but it shouldn't get so dry that it sticks.

3. Once the meat is tender and almost falling apart, remove the lid and reduce the sauce, if necessary – vindaloo should have a thick, rich gravy. Taste as you go, and add more chilli flakes or powder, if needed.

4. Stir through the tamarind at the end of cooking. Serve with freshly cooked rice, plus poppadoms and pickles.

Lamb Rogan Josh

We first published this recipe in 'Happy Curries', back in 2019. Often, we tweak recipes over the years, but this has stood the test of time, and we still make it the same way as our original version.

PREP TIME 10 MINUTES + MARINATING • COOK TIME 50 MINUTES

SoF / NF / WF / GF • SERVES 4

- 800g (1lb 12oz) boneless lamb shoulder, cut into bite-sized chunks, fat trimmed off
- 5 heaped tablespoons plain yoghurt
- 4cm (1½in) piece of ginger, peeled and finely grated
- ½ teaspoon hot chilli powder, plus 2 teaspoons paprika or 1 tablespoon Kashmiri chilli powder
- 1 tablespoon neutral oil or ghee, for cooking
- ¼ teaspoon ground mace
- ½ teaspoon asafoetida
- 5 cloves
- seeds from 4 cardamom pods
- ½ teaspoon fennel seeds
- pinch of saffron
- 250ml (9fl oz) hot water
- salt and freshly ground black pepper
- coriander leaves, to garnish

TO SERVE:
- freshly cooked rice (allow 60–75g /2¼–2¾oz uncooked rice person)
- warmed Indian breads

1. Place the lamb in a bowl with the yoghurt, ginger, chilli powder and paprika plus a generous pinch of salt. Mix to coat the lamb, then cover and leave in the fridge for at least 20 minutes, but ideally overnight.

2. When ready to cook, pour the oil into a large, deep pan over a medium heat. When hot, add the lamb and all its marinade, stirring regularly and letting the meat brown lightly all over and the marinade reduce.

3. Meanwhile, using a spice grinder or mortar and pestle, grind all the spices until smooth and well mixed. Turn the heat to low and add the spices to the pan. Cook, stirring often, for about 10 minutes, until really fragrant.

4. Soak the saffron in the hot water for about 5 minutes, then pour the whole lot into the pan. Bring up to a gentle simmer, then cover and leave to bubble gently for about 20 minutes. The gravy will still be quite thin, so remove the lid and heat rapidly for a further 10 minutes, stirring to prevent sticking, until reduced by about half.

5. Serve with rice and breads, and the fresh coriander leaves sprinkled over.

Lamb Dhansak

Although the Parsi version of this dish always contains meat, you can make it vegetarian by swapping the meat for cooked chickpeas and chunks of aubergine, and cooking it for about 25 minutes in the oven. Because it cooks low and slow, dhansak is often served for Sunday lunch and at family celebrations. If you've ever had dhansak made with pineapple, that's a (slightly baffling) British curry-house addition to the original recipe.

PREP TIME 25 MINUTES • COOK TIME 2 HOURS

SoF / DF / NF • SERVES 4

- 50g (1¾oz) urid dal (split black lentils)
- 50g (1¾oz) split red lentils
- 50g (1¾oz) brown lentils
- 1 litre (1¾ pints) hot water
- 1 tablespoon neutral oil
- 2 onions, finely chopped
- 4 cloves of garlic, crushed or finely grated
- 4cm (1½in) piece of ginger, peeled and finely grated
- 800g (1lb 12oz) diced lamb shoulder meat
- 100g (3½oz) fresh tomatoes, chopped
- 1 small sweet potato or about 150g (5½oz) pumpkin, peeled and diced
- 1 tablespoon finely chopped fresh green chilli
- 1 tablespoon finely chopped fresh dill
- 1 tablespoon roughly chopped fresh mint leaves
- 1 tablespoon roughly chopped fresh coriander leaves, plus extra to garnish
- 1 tablespoon tamarind paste, from a jar
- 50g (1¾oz) frozen fenugreek (methi) leaves, or 1 heaped tablespoon dried fenugreek leaves (optional)
- ½ teaspoon salt, or to taste
- rice or flatbreads (WF / GF if needed), to serve

1. Wash all the lentils under cold running water, and pick over to remove any debris. Fill a large pan with the hot water, add the lentils and bring to a fast boil. Skim off any scum and, after about 5 minutes, turn the heat down, cover and simmer for 25 minutes. (A pressure cooker, if you have one, can be used to speed up the cooking.)

2. Meanwhile, set a large, deep, ovenproof pan over a medium heat. Add the oil and when hot, add the onions. Cook, stirring often, until they begin to brown a little, about 6–8 minutes.

3. Now make the spice mixture: using a spice grinder or mortar and pestle, grind the whole spices together, then add the ground spices and mix well.

4. Heat the oven to 140°C/325°F/gas mark 3.

5. Add the garlic, ginger and spice mixture to the onion pan and cook for 2 minutes, stirring. Now add the lamb and cook, still stirring, for 5 minutes, just until it takes on a little colour. Add the tomatoes and cook for a further 5 minutes, stirring now and then. Once they have broken down a little, add the sweet potato, fresh chilli, fresh dill, mint and coriander (saving a little of each herb to garnish), then the tamarind and fenugreek leaves, if using.

6. Carefully ladle the contents of the lentil pan into the onion pan. If it seems dry, add a touch more water. Bring back to a simmer, then cover with a lid and place in the oven for 1

FOR THE SPICE MIXTURE:
- ½ teaspoon coriander seeds
- ¼ teaspoon cumin seeds
- seeds from 3 cardamom pods
- 3 cloves
- ½ teaspoon fennel seeds
- pinch of fenugreek seeds
- ¼ teaspoon ground cinnamon
- ½ teaspoon ground turmeric
- ½ teaspoon chilli powder, or 1 teaspoon Kashmiri chilli powder, which is milder
- pinch of freshly grated nutmeg
- ¼ teaspoon ground ginger
- pinch of freshly ground black pepper

hour, keeping an eye on liquid levels, and checking to see if the lamb needs any longer – it should be falling apart when cooked. Return to the oven if necessary for 15–30 minutes, until it's ready.

7. Remove the lamb from the oven. To thicken the gravy, scoop 4 ladlefuls of the lentils, vegetables and broth into a blender and blitz until smooth, then return to the pan. If it still seems a little thin, place on the hob over a medium-high heat and let it bubble to reduce further.

8. Add ¼ teaspoon of salt, then taste and decide if you want to add more – we use about ½ teaspoon in total. You can also add more chilli for heat, or tamarind for sourness.

9. Serve with rice or flatbreads.

→ *Pictured overleaf*

TIP

Mutton is wonderful in this recipe, though it needs a longer cooking time, and is much harder to find than lamb.

Ashley's Spiced Chicken Pittas

Ashley Davis from LEON's HQ says this is her favourite easy summer lunch to make for friends.

PREP TIME 20 MINUTES + MARINATING • COOK TIME 25 MINUTES

SoF / NF • SERVES 4

- 2 tablespoons olive oil
- 1 tablespoon freshly squeezed lemon juice, plus extra to serve
- ½ teaspoon ground cumin
- ½ teaspoon ground coriander
- ½ teaspoon onion powder
- ½ teaspoon ground turmeric
- ¼ teaspoon ground cinnamon
- 1 teaspoon paprika
- 1 tablespoon LEON chilli ketchup, or 1 tablespoon tomato ketchup plus ¼ teaspoon cayenne pepper and ¼ teaspoon smoked paprika
- 1 small clove of garlic, crushed
- 800g (1lb 12oz) boneless, skin-on chicken thighs
- fine salt and freshly ground black pepper

TO SERVE:
- 6 warmed pittas, halved and split open
- pomegranate seeds, coriander leaves, shredded lettuce, Pink Kraut (see page 192) or pickled cabbage, sliced cucumbers, Greek-style plain yoghurt or Tzatziki (see page 33)

1. Place the oil and lemon juice in a large bowl, add the spices, ketchup, garlic and a good twist of salt and pepper. Mix well.

2. Place the chicken on a board and use a sharp knife to make a few small slits through the skin and into the meat. Place in the marinade and rub it in, then cover and leave in the fridge for at least 1 hour, but ideally overnight.

3. When ready to cook, heat the oven to 180°C/400°F/gas mark 6. Line a roasting tray with baking parchment.

4. Arrange the chicken in the prepared tray and roast for 20–25 minutes, basting once halfway through, or until the skin is dark brown and crisp, and the meat is cooked through. (Check by piercing a thigh with the tip of a knife – there should be no pink juices.)

5. Squeeze a little lemon juice over the thighs, then set aside to rest for 5 minutes.

6. To serve, slice the chicken into bite-sized pieces and tuck inside the pittas, along with some pomegranate seeds, coriander leaves, shredded lettuce, Pink Kraut, pickled cucumber and a spoonful of yoghurt or Tzatziki. Serve each person with 3 pitta halves and eat straight away.

Pulled Duck Tacos & Pineapple Chilli Sauce

Sweet-but-sour pineapple – as it turns out – makes a brilliant hot sauce, which goes really well with crispy, salty shredded duck. Be sure to use high-welfare duck legs for this dish and don't be tempted to discard the skin, first because it protects the meat during cooking and second because, fried until crisp, it makes a wonderful garnish for the tacos, much like Mexican chicharrónes (which is made with pork skin).

PREP TIME 25 MINUTES • COOK TIME 1 HOUR 15 MINUTES

SoF / NF / GF / WF / DF • SERVES 4

- 4 duck legs
- ½ teaspoon fine sea salt, plus extra to season

FOR THE ROAST PINEAPPLE CHILLI SAUCE:
- ½ pineapple, peeled and cored, then cut into large chunks (about 400g/14oz)
- 1 head of garlic, halved horizontally through the middle
- 2 whole red chillies, or more if you like heat
- ½ red onion
- 1 yellow pepper, halved
- 1 teaspoon chipotle chilli flakes
- 1 tablespoon cider vinegar
- juice of ½ lime
- ¾ teaspoon fine salt

TO SERVE:
- pure corn tortillas, sliced radishes, shredded white cabbage or crisp lettuce, sliced red chillies (optional), finely sliced shallot dressed with lime juice, coriander leaves

1. Heat the oven to 180°C/400°F/gas mark 6. Set out a large metal roasting tray with a good-sized rim.

2. Pat the duck legs dry with kitchen paper, then season the underside with half the salt. Place in the tray skin-side up and sprinkle with the remaining salt. Add the chunks of pineapple to the tray, along with the garlic, chillies, red onion and yellow pepper. Don't add any fat at this point as the duck will produce enough.

3. Roast for 15 minutes, then baste just the fruit and veg (not the duck). Roast for another 30 minutes, then remove the chillies and garlic, set them aside, and baste everything else, including the duck. Roast for a further 15 minutes, then remove the pepper and onion, which should be soft and slightly charred. Set aside to cool with the chillies and garlic. Roast the meat and the pineapple for another 15 minutes (the meat needs a total of 1¼ hours). Set both aside to cool a little.

4. Chop the pineapple roughly, then place in a blender with all the other sauce ingredients and blitz until completely smooth. Add enough cold water to make a spoonable sauce. Taste to check it has a sweet and sour heat from the chipotle. Add more salt, chipotle or lime juice, as needed. Set aside.

5. When the meat has cooled a little, pull off the skin, keeping it in large pieces if possible. Spoon a little of the duck fat into a frying pan over a medium heat and fry the duck skin gently, until very crisp but not burnt. Lift out with a slotted spoon and pat dry with kitchen paper. Chop the skin into small pieces. It should taste salty, so if not, add a pinch of fine salt and toss again. Set aside.

6. Using two forks, pull the meat from the duck legs and shred it. Keep warm. (If the meat cools, reheat with a splash of water in a small pan before serving.)

7. To serve, warm the tortillas and get the garnishes ready. Pile a little of the duck onto a tortilla, then spoon over some of the pineapple sauce and a sprinkling of crisp duck skin. Add some sliced radish, shredded cabbage or lettuce, shallot, coriander leaves and red chilli, if using. Serve the remaining sauce on the side and eat straight away.

↦ *Pictured overleaf*

TIP

Don't hold back on the pineapple hot sauce – it will only keep for 3–4 days in the fridge.

Sweet & Sticky Pork Bao Buns

Plump little bao buns, also known as steamed buns, are fluffy and sweet, but are traditionally filled with savoury ingredients. Here we stuff them with barbecue-style pork and a sweet-spicy sauce.

PREP TIME 25 MINUTES PLUS MARINATING • COOK TIME 30 MINUTES

NF • SERVES 4

- 1kg (2lb 4oz) pork shoulder
- 12 ready-made bao buns, warmed

FOR THE MARINADE:
- 2 teaspoons dark brown sugar
- 2 teaspoons Chinese five-spice
- 3 tablespoons Shaoxing rice wine
- 3 tablespoons soy sauce
- 2 tablespoons hoisin sauce
- ¼ teaspoon white pepper
- ½ teaspoon fine salt
- ½ teaspoon garlic powder
- 1 tablespoon runny honey

FOR THE SAUCE:
- 2 teaspoons sweet chilli sauce
- 2 teaspoons hoisin sauce

TO SERVE:
- finely sliced spring onion, cucumber and red chilli, crispy onions (from a packet), coriander leaves, 2 tablespoons finely chopped salted peanuts

1. Cut the pork into pieces, about 4cm (1½in) wide. Use the tip of a sharp knife to make small incisions all over the pork. Place all the marinade ingredients, except the honey, in a bowl or sealable plastic bag and mix until smooth. Add the pork and massage the marinade into it. Cover or seal, and place in the fridge for at least 8 hours, but ideally overnight.

2. When ready to cook, heat the oven to 220°C/475°F/gas mark 9. Line a roasting tray with a single sheet of foil.

3. Using a slotted spoon, transfer the pork from the marinade to the prepared tray. Place the meat in the oven for 15 minutes. Meanwhile, whisk the honey into the remaining marinade to make a glaze.

4. When the 15 minutes are up, turn the meat, which should be lightly charring at the edges, and brush with the glaze. Return to the oven for 8 minutes. Turn the meat and brush with the glaze again, then cook for another 5 minutes.

5. Transfer the meat and cooking juices to a clean bowl and cover with foil. Set aside to rest for 10 minutes.

6. Meanwhile, warm the buns according to the packet instructions, opening them out gently, and prepare the other fillings. Stir the sauce ingredients together.

7. Slice the meat into thin strips, then tuck it into the buns with a little of the sauce and some of each filling. Eat straight away.

TIP

Bao buns are available in larger supermarkets. Leftover meat can be used the next day with fried rice or noodles.

Blackened Trout Tacos
with Ají Verde

We love our ají verde, a green chilli-based sauce – it works brilliantly with fish, but can also be spooned over grilled chicken, tacos, or even in a burrito-style wrap.

PREP TIME 20 MINUTES • COOK TIME 8 MINUTES

SoF / NF / WF / GF • SERVES 4

- 70g (2½oz) radishes, finely sliced
- 125g (4½oz) red cabbage, shredded
- 2 spring onions, finely sliced
- ½ avocado, diced
- 1 red chilli, finely sliced
- a generous handful of coriander leaves
- a squeeze of lime juice, plus wedges to serve
- 2–3 pure corn tortillas per person

FOR THE AJÍ VERDE SAUCE:
- 3 tablespoons mayonnaise
- 3 tablespoons soured cream
- a big handful of coriander leaves, chopped
- a small handful of flat leaf parsley leaves, chopped
- ½ green chilli, finely chopped
- 2 teaspoons finely chopped jalapeños
- 1 teaspoon cider vinegar
- 1 teaspoon lime juice
- 1 small clove of garlic, crushed
- salt and freshly ground black pepper

FOR THE FISH:
- ½ teaspoon chilli powder
- 1 teaspoon paprika
- 1 teaspoon ground cumin
- ½ teaspoon ground coriander
- 1 teaspoon garlic or onion powder
- 3–4 skinless trout fillets
- rapeseed oil, for cooking

1. Prepare the vegetables and herbs for the filling. Place in a serving bowl, but keep each ingredient separate. Squeeze some lime juice over the cabbage, radishes and avocado. Set aside.

2. Put the sauce ingredients into a blender and blitz together until smooth. It should be spicy, tart and creamy, so taste and adjust the salt, pepper and lime as needed.

3. Combine the fish spices and a pinch of salt in a bowl. Dust both sides of each trout fillet with the mixture to coat evenly.

4. Pour a splash of cooking oil into a frying pan over a medium heat. When hot, add the fish and cook for about 3 minutes per side, or until just cooked through – thicker fillets might take slightly longer, and you might need to turn them a couple of times to stop the spices burning. When the spices have formed a dark crust on both sides, transfer the fish to a warmed plate.

5. Briefly warm the tortillas in a low oven or in the microwave. Wrap the stack in a clean tea towel to keep warm.

6. To serve, break the fish into large pieces and place some on each tortilla. Top with a handful of the prepared vegetables and herbs, followed by a generous drizzle of the sauce. Fold loosely in half to eat and serve with the remaining sauce.

Deep-Dish Lasagne

It's worth making more of this than you'll eat on the day because the rest can be frozen for future meals. Using pork as well as beef in the meat sauce is traditional in Italy, and makes for a particularly tender ragu.

PREP TIME 20 MINUTES • COOK TIME 2 HOURS

SoF / NF • SERVES 6

- olive oil, for cooking and brushing
- 500g (1lb 2oz) minced beef
- 500g (1lb 2oz) minced pork
- 1 onion, finely diced
- 1 large carrot, finely diced
- 2 celery sticks, finely diced
- 1 smoked bacon rasher, finely diced
- 2 tablespoons tomato purée
- 3 cloves of garlic, crushed
- 300ml (10fl oz) red wine
- 500ml (18fl oz) hot beef stock
- 100ml (3½fl oz) milk
- 2 bay leaves
- 2 teaspoons chopped fresh thyme leaves
- 1 teaspoon finely chopped fresh rosemary
- 12–15 dried lasagne sheets, depending on dish size and shape
- salt and freshly ground black pepper

FOR THE CHEESE SAUCE:
- 100g (3½oz) salted butter
- 100g (3½oz) plain flour
- 800ml (28fl oz) milk
- 25g (1oz) Parmesan cheese, finely grated, plus extra for sprinkling
- a generous pinch of freshly grated nutmeg
- 1 × 125g (4½oz) ball of mozzarella cheese, torn into strips
- salt and pepper (ideally white pepper)

1. Place a wide, heavy-based pan over a medium heat and add a splash of olive oil. When hot, brown the beef first and then the pork, in batches. Set aside the browned meat and add a little more oil to the pan. Add the onion, carrot, celery and bacon and sauté for 8–10 minutes, stirring often, until the onion is translucent and beginning to brown. Add the tomato purée and garlic and cook for a couple of minutes, again stirring often, then add the wine, stock, milk, bay leaves, thyme and rosemary. Season with a pinch of salt and some freshly ground pepper. Bring to a simmer, cover with a lid and leave to cook for 1 hour. Remove the lid and allow the sauce to reduce for about 20 minutes, but don't make it too dry – it should be wetter than a bolognese-type sauce, as much of the liquid will be absorbed by the pasta sheets.

2. While the ragu simmers, make the cheese sauce. Melt the butter in a large saucepan over a medium heat, then add the flour. Stir to form a golden paste, and continue stirring constantly for a minute or so. Turn the heat to low and begin to add the milk, 2 tablespoons at a time, stirring as you do so, or the sauce will become lumpy. When about 300ml (10fl oz) of the milk has been added, and the sauce is thick and smooth, you can add it more quickly. Turn the heat to medium and cook the sauce, stirring every minute or so for about 10 minutes, until it begins to thicken. Add the Parmesan, a generous dusting of freshly grated nutmeg and some salt and white pepper (if you have it). Taste and adjust the seasoning as necessary.

3. Heat the oven to 200°C/425°F/gas mark 7. Brush a large baking dish (about 20 × 30cm/8 × 12in) with olive oil.

4. The lasagne will need five layers of both ragu and cheese sauce, and four layers of pasta. Start by spooning a layer of ragu into the prepared dish, then a layer of cheese sauce. Cover with lasagne sheets, slightly overlapping, then repeat the layers, finishing with a layer of cheese sauce. Arrange the mozzarella on top, then grate extra Parmesan over the surface. Bake for 25 minutes, or until the lasagne is bubbling and golden brown. Leave to stand for 5–10 minutes before serving.

Six-Hour Oxtail Ragu

Rather than speedily smashing together a few high-octane foodstuffs, the big flavours of this extraordinarily rich and savoury ragu come from a low and slow combination of simple ingredients.

PREP TIME 20 MINUTES • COOK TIME 6¾ HOURS

SoF / NF • SERVES 6–8

- olive oil, for cooking
- 1.2kg (2lb 10oz) oxtail (with bone), cut into large pieces
- 75g (2¾oz) pancetta or guanciale, finely chopped
- 1 onion, finely diced
- 1 celery stick, finely diced
- 1 carrot, finely diced
- 3 cloves of garlic, crushed
- 1 tablespoon tomato purée
- 2 sprigs of rosemary
- 2 bay leaves
- 500g (1lb 2oz) tomato passata
- about 600ml (20fl oz) hot chicken stock
- 2 tablespoons white wine vinegar
- 80–100g/2¾–3½oz dried pappardelle, or 120g/4¼oz fresh egg pappardelle per person (or a WF / GF alternative)
- salt and freshly ground black pepper
- freshly grated Parmesan cheese, to serve

TIP

Since this dish cooks for such a long time, it's worth making in large quantities, as we have here; it freezes brilliantly and tastes even better the next day.

1. Set a large, heavy-based pan over a high heat. Add a splash of oil, and when hot use tongs to arrange the oxtail pieces in it in a single layer. Sear each piece on all sides until really well browned (a splash guard is useful, if you have one, as a lot of fat may mist upwards). Transfer the oxtail to a plate, then lower the heat under the pan and add a little more oil, if needed. Add the pancetta and cook for 6–8 minutes, stirring occasionally, until golden. Now add the vegetables and leave to sweat for about 8 minutes, stirring every so often. (Lower the heat further if the veg start to brown too fast or burn.) Add the garlic and tomato purée and sauté, stirring all the time, for another minute or so.

2. Pop the rosemary and bay leaves in the pan, then pour in the passata, stock and vinegar. Stir well. Bring to a simmer, cover with a lid and leave on a low heat, just bubbling, for about 6 hours. Stir occasionally and top up with hot water as needed.

3. The meat is ready when it begins to fall off the bones. If there is a lot of fat on the surface of the ragu, spoon some off. Lift the oxtail from the pan and gently pull the meat from the bones with 2 forks, discarding any cartilage and fragments of bone. Return the meat to the pan and cook for a few minutes longer, stirring and allowing the meat to incorporate into the sauce. Taste and season with salt and pepper, if needed.

4. Cook the pasta until al dente, then drain and toss in a splash of olive oil to prevent sticking. Divide between wide shallow serving bowls and top with the ragu and a little freshly grated Parmesan, plus more at the table.

Brown Crab Cacio E Pepe

Rebecca thought she'd come up with this by herself, but then discovered it on the menu at a London restaurant called Manteca. She'd never encountered it before, so the idea must have been in the air.

PREP TIME 15 MINUTES • COOK TIME 12 MINUTES

SoF / NF • SERVES 4

- 400g (14oz) dried pasta (linguine or spaghetti work best)
- 100g (3½oz) brown crab meat (don't worry if a little white meat finds its way in too)
- 2 tablespoons cold water
- ½ teaspoon finely ground black pepper
- 60g (2¼oz) salted butter
- lemon juice, to taste
- finely grated Parmesan cheese, to taste

1. Bring a large pan of salted water to the boil and cook the pasta until al dente, or one minute less than the packet suggests.

2. Meanwhile, put the crab meat and measured water into a blender or food processor and pulse until fairly smooth. (If you prefer, use a bowl and a stick blender.)

3. Place a small frying pan over a medium–low heat and add the pepper, toasting it for 1–2 minutes, just until fragrant. Add the butter and, once it is bubbling, add 5 tablespoons of the starchy pasta water.

4. When the pasta is done, drain, reserving a mugful of the pasta cooking water, then return the pasta to the pan. Place back over a low heat and pour in the butter mixture. Toss briskly, letting the sauce emulsify with the starch from the pasta. Remove from the heat and add the crab meat, a squeeze of lemon juice and a handful of Parmesan. Toss well to emulsify again, then taste. If the sauce seems dry, add a spoonful of the reserved pasta water, plus more lemon or Parmesan as needed. Serve in wide bowls.

TIP

Both brown and white crab meat can be frozen, so nothing need go to waste if a particular recipe requires just one type. The white crab meat is great for making crab cakes.

Smoked Mackerel Potato Ravioli

Potato ravioli is a traditional pasta from Tuscany. We've amped things up by adding smoked mackerel, and slathering it in a brown butter, lemon and dill sauce.

PREP TIME 45 MINUTES + RESTING/CHILLING • COOK TIME 30 MINUTES

SoF / NF • SERVES 4

- 200g (7oz) 'oo' flour, plus extra for kneading, rolling and dusting
- 2 eggs, lightly beaten, plus 2 egg yolks for later
- 250g (9oz) floury white potatoes
- 50g (1¾oz) butter, melted
- 3 smoked mackerel fillets, skin and bones removed, flesh very finely shredded
- 1 small clove of garlic, crushed to a paste
- 2 tablespoons very finely chopped flat leaf parsley
- a pinch of freshly grated nutmeg
- zest and juice from 1 unwaxed lemon (see Tip, page 82)
- sea salt and freshly ground black pepper

FOR THE SAUCE:
- 100g (3½oz) butter, cut into cubes
- lemon zest and juice, to taste
- 3 tablespoons finely chopped dill

1. Place the flour in a bowl and make a well in the centre. Pour in the beaten eggs and use a spoon to gradually work the flour into them. Once you have a rough, claggy dough, shape into a ball, then knead it on a clean floured surface for at least 5 minutes, or until the dough starts to feel smooth and stretchy (or use a mixer with a dough hook). Cover the dough with a small bowl or with clingfilm and set aside for about 30 minutes.

2. Meanwhile, place the whole unpeeled potatoes in a pan of boiling water and cook until tender, about 15–20 minutes. Drain, cool, then peel off the skins and leave the potatoes to steam dry for a couple of minutes. Mash thoroughly (a potato ricer is best for this). Add the remaining ingredients, season with lots of salt and pepper, and mix until well combined. Taste and add more salt and lemon, if needed. Add the egg yolks and mix again. Place in the fridge for 20 minutes.

3. Once the dough has rested, divide it into 8 equal pieces and shape into small rectangles. Dust a clean work surface with flour (or use a pasta rolling machine) and roll each piece of dough into a rectangle about 60 × 20cm (24 × 8in) and 2mm (⅟₁₆in) thick. The dough needs to be really thin, as it will thicken up once it hits the cooking water. Lay the 8 pasta sheets out on the floury work surface and cover with a clean tea towel to prevent them from drying out.

4. Line a couple of baking trays with nonstick baking paper and dust with flour.

5. Dot tablespoons of the filling on four of the pasta sheets, spacing them about 3cm (1¼in) apart. Press each mound

→ *Pictured overleaf*

slightly to flatten it to the width of a 50p coin (about 25mm/1in), then brush water around each one. Lie another sheet of pasta on top and, working from the centre outwards, gently press the pasta together, pushing out the air around the mounds of filling. Use a ravioli cutter or sharp knife to cut out 'parcels' about 6cm (2½in) square (if using a knife, take extra care to press the sealed edges together). Set the finished parcels on the floured baking tray. If you have lots of pasta and filling left, reroll the dough to make more ravioli, or use the offcuts to make tagliatelle, which you can dry and store in the fridge.

6. To make the sauce, place a small pan over a medium heat and add the butter. Once foaming, watch closely until the foaming dies down and the milk solids start to brown. As it can quickly burn at this point, tip the butter into a small bowl to cool slightly.

7. Place a large pan of well-salted, freshly boiled water over a high heat. When boiling, lower the heat to a simmer and gently add the ravioli. (You might need to do this in two batches, unless your pan is big enough to fit it all with plenty of room.) Cook for 3–4 minutes, turning the pasta once. Using a slotted spoon, drain the ravioli and transfer to warmed serving bowls.

8. Meanwhile, add a pinch of the lemon zest and some juice to the warm brown butter. Taste and add more lemon and salt, if needed. Mix well, as the caramelized parts will sink, then spoon the sauce over the ravioli. Sprinkle with the chopped dill and a little more lemon zest before serving.

TIP

For extra piquancy, add a few finely diced capers to the sauce just before serving.

Four-Cheese Mac & Cheese

The only thing better than macaroni cheese is macaroni cheese made with extra cheese

PREP TIME 15 MINUTES • COOK TIME 55 MINUTES

SoF / NF / V • SERVES 6

- 500g (1lb 2oz) dried macaroni
- olive oil or butter, for greasing

FOR THE CHEESE SAUCE:
- 100g (3½oz) salted butter
- 75g (2¾oz) plain flour
- 1.3 litres (2¼ pints) milk
- pinch of freshly grated nutmeg
- ¼ teaspoon (or more) English mustard powder, to taste
- a pinch of cayenne pepper (optional)
- 225g (8oz) Cheddar cheese, grated
- 110g (3¾oz) Parmesan cheese, finely grated (check V, if needed)
- 100g (3½oz) Swiss cheese or Gruyère, grated (check V, if needed)
- 1 × 125g (4½oz) ball mozzarella cheese, torn into pieces
- ground pepper (preferably white), to taste

1. Cook the macaroni in a large pan of boiling salted water for 6 minutes, or until al dente. Drain and toss in a little olive oil, to prevent sticking.

2. Meanwhile, in a separate large deep pan, melt the butter over a medium heat, then turn the heat to low and stir in the flour, until a golden paste forms. Continue to cook and stir for 2 minutes. Now start to add the milk, a few spoonfuls at a time, mixing well each time – this will help to prevent lumps. Repeat this process until you've added about 300ml (10fl oz) of the milk and have a thick, smooth sauce; you can now pour in the rest more quickly. Stir until completely smooth again, then add the nutmeg, mustard powder (breaking up any lumps, or someone will get a punchy surprise), cayenne pepper and a pinch of white pepper. Cook, stirring often, for about 10 minutes. It will start off looking very thin, but will thicken and become silkier. Turn the heat right down and add 100g (3½oz) of the Cheddar, 65g of the Parmesan and all the Swiss cheese, then stir briskly until melted. Remove from the heat – if the cheese gets too hot, it will split and make the sauce grainy – then taste. It probably won't need salt, but you can add more mustard powder if you like.

3. Heat the oven to 200°C/425°F/gas mark 7. Grease a large baking dish (about 20 × 30cm/8 × 12in) with the oil or butter.

4. Tip the cooked macaroni into the sauce and mix well. Pour half the mac mixture into the prepared dish and dot with the mozzarella pieces. Pour over the rest of the macaroni, then top with the remaining Cheddar and Parmesan. Bake for 20 minutes, or until bubbling and golden brown.

TIP

For a five-cheese mac, add half the mixture to the baking dish, then add a layer of wilted and drained spinach (about 150g/5½oz) and a handful of crumbled blue cheese, before adding the rest as described above.

Kimchi Mac & Cheese

Rebecca has been obsessed with combining cheese, chilli and kimchi ever since trying Korean-Mexican street food in LA more than a decade ago. This combination is always a good idea.

PREP TIME 15 MINUTES • COOK TIME 55 MINUTES

NF / V • SERVES 6

- 500g (1lb 2oz) dried macaroni
- a splash of olive oil

FOR THE CHEESE AND KIMCHI SAUCE:
- 100g (3½oz) salted butter
- 75g (2¾oz) plain flour
- 1.3 litres (2¼ pints) milk
- 175g (6oz) Cheddar cheese, grated
- 3 tablespoons gochujang (Korean chilli paste), or more to taste
- 2 heaped tablespoons kimchi (shop-bought or see page 194 for homemade), drained and finely chopped (V if needed)
- 6 spring onions, trimmed, halved lengthways and finely chopped
- 1 red chilli, finely chopped, plus more to taste
- 1 × 125g (4½oz) ball of mozzarella cheese, torn into pieces
- 50g (1¾oz) panko breadcrumbs
- neutral cooking oil

1. Cook the macaroni in a large pan of boiling salted water for 6 minutes, or until al dente. Drain and toss in a little olive oil.

2. Meanwhile, in a separate large deep pan, melt the butter over a medium heat. Turn the heat to low and stir in the flour, until a golden paste forms. Continue to cook and stir for 2 minutes. Now start to add the milk, a few spoonfuls at a time, mixing well each time to prevent lumps developing. Repeat this process until you've added about 300ml (10fl oz) of the milk and have a thick, smooth sauce; you can now pour in the rest. Stir until completely smooth again, then cook, stirring often, for about 10 minutes. It will start off looking very thin, but will thicken and become silkier. Turn the heat right down, add 125g (4½oz) of the Cheddar and stir briskly until melted. Remove from the heat – if the cheese gets too hot it will split and make the sauce grainy. Add the gochujang, kimchi, spring onions and chilli. Taste and add more gochujang or fresh chilli, if liked.

3. Heat the oven to 200°C/425°F/gas mark 7. Grease a large baking dish (about 20 × 30cm/8 × 12in) with the cooking oil.

4. Tip the cooked macaroni into the sauce and mix well. Pour half the mac mixture into the prepared dish and dot with the mozzarella pieces. Pour over the rest of the macaroni and sprinkle with the remaining 50g (1¾oz) Cheddar.

5. Place the breadcrumbs in a bowl, add a splash of cooking oil and toss to combine. Sprinkle over the macaroni and bake for 20–25 minutes, or until the top is bubbling and the breadcrumbs are crisp and golden brown. Leave to stand for 5 minutes before serving.

Crispy Gnocchi & Squash

It's best to use gnocchi from the fridge section of the supermarket for this, rather than the vacuum-packed ones on the shelf, as they are a little softer and fry up better.

PREP TIME 20 MINUTES • COOK TIME 45 MINUTES

SoF / WF / GF / V • SERVES 2

- 1 butternut squash, peeled, seeded and cut into 3cm (1¼in) chunks
- 1 onion, cut into 6 chunks
- 1 head of garlic, halved across the middle
- 3 tablespoons olive oil
- a handful of walnuts, roughly chopped
- 2 tablespoons pumpkin seeds
- 75ml (2½fl oz) double cream
- 2 heaped tablespoons freshly grated Parmesan cheese, plus extra to serve (check V, if needed)
- 1½ tablespoons olive oil
- a generous knob of butter
- 250g (9oz) ready-made gnocchi (check WF / GF if needed)
- a handful of sage leaves
- salt and freshly ground black pepper

1. Heat the oven to 200°C/425°F/gas mark 7.
2. Place the squash in a rimmed baking tray along with the onion and garlic. Spoon over the olive oil and gently toss with your hands to coat each piece completely, but without letting the onion wedges fall apart. Roast for 30 minutes.
3. Meanwhile, gently toast the walnut pieces and pumpkin seeds in a hot, dry frying pan until the seeds pop and the walnuts smell fragrant. Transfer to a plate and set aside.
4. Remove the tray from the oven, sprinkle over a generous pinch of salt and use a spoon to turn the vegetables and break up the onion. Return to the oven for 5 minutes, then set aside. When cool enough to handle, carefully pop the garlic cloves out of their skins. Discard any leathery bits of onion.
5. Place the roasted vegetables, cream, Parmesan and some black pepper in a blender or food processor and blitz until fairly smooth. Taste and season with more salt, pepper or Parmesan. If the mixture is very thick, add a splash more cream – it should be spoonable, not stiff. Keep warm.
6. Place a large frying pan over a medium heat and add the oil and butter. Once foaming, tip the gnocchi in and fry for about 3 minutes on each side, until deep golden all over.
7. Spoon the squash purée into warm serving bowls and spread out slightly. Divide the fried gnocchi between the portions. Add the sage leaves to the hot oil remaining in the pan and fry for a minute or so. Scatter the seeds and nuts over the gnocchi, then grate or shave more Parmesan over the top. Finish with the crisp sage leaves and eat straight away.

Carne Asada

Carne asada is a Mexican-style way to marinate and then grill beef, before slicing it thinly. The marinade is deliciously fiery so we make it go further by adding roasted peppers to make a sauce.

PREP TIME 20 MINUTES + MARINATING • COOK TIME 16 MINUTES

WF / GF / NF / DF • SERVES 4

- 900g (2lb) skirt steak, cut into 2 pieces 4–5 cm (1½–2in) thick, patted dry with kitchen paper
- 1 teaspoon cumin seeds
- 1 teaspoon coriander seeds
- juice of 2 oranges
- juice of 2 limes
- 1 tablespoon olive oil
- 1 tablespoon chipotle chilli flakes
- 1 teaspoon soy sauce (WF / GF if needed)
- 1 teaspoon fish sauce
- ½ teaspoon fine salt
- ½ teaspoon ground cumin
- 1 teaspoon brown sugar
- 4 cloves of garlic, roughly chopped
- 1 tablespoon finely chopped jalapeño chillies from a jar
- a pinch of freshly ground black pepper
- a pinch of dried oregano
- 2 roasted red peppers, from a jar (in oil, not brine or vinegar)
- neutral oil, for cooking

TO SERVE:
- tomato and sliced red onion salad, dressed in lime juice
- steamed rice mixed with cooked black beans
- Grilled Corn Salad (see page 52)

1. Place the steak in a large dish. Lightly bruise the cumin and coriander seeds in a mortar, then place them and all the other ingredients, apart from the red peppers and cooking oil, in a blender (or use a stick blender) and blitz until smooth. Pour half this marinade over the beef and use your hands to massage it into the meat on all sides. Cover and marinate in the fridge for at least 4 hours, but ideally overnight.

2. Add the roasted peppers to the remaining unused marinade and blitz again to form a hot sauce. Pour into a jug, cover and store in the fridge until needed.

3. An hour before you want to cook, get the meat out of the fridge.

4. When ready to cook, place a large frying pan over a very high heat. When really hot, add a tablespoon of oil and swirl it all over the pan and up the sides. Remove the steak from the marinade, letting the excess drain back into the dish. Place the meat in the pan and, if you have one, put a splash guard over the top and turn on the extractor fan or open a window. Sear the meat hard for 6–8 minutes a side, as it's thick and will probably take longer than you expect to get the meat beyond blue to rare, and to develop a dark, spicy crust. (If you press the meat with your finger and it is very soft and yielding, it is still very rare – beef firms up as it cooks.)

5. Transfer the meat to a board to rest for about 10 minutes, loosely covered with foil. Finish preparing any sides.

6. To serve, use a very sharp or serrated knife to cut the meat into slices 1cm (½in) thick, going against the grain. Serve with the hot sauce and side dishes

Caramel Pork
with Garlicky Greens

This dish is our homage to Vietnamese caramel pork, a beautifully sweet and savoury dish that is traditionally served with home-fermented mustard greens – but we've swapped them for garlicky steamed greens here.

PREP TIME 20 MINUTES • **COOK TIME 1 HOUR 25 MINUTES**

SoF / NF / WF / GF / DF • **SERVES 4**

- neutral oil, for cooking
- 500g (1lb 2oz) pork shoulder, cut into 3cm (1¼in) chunks
- 1 small onion or 2 shallots, finely sliced
- 1 teaspoon brown sugar
- ½ teaspoon garlic powder
- ½ teaspoon fine salt and lots of freshly ground black pepper
- 2 teaspoons fish sauce, plus extra if needed
- 500ml (18fl oz) coconut water
- 4 eggs

FOR THE CARAMEL:
- 3 tablespoons caster sugar
- 100ml (3½fl oz) water

FOR THE GREENS:
- 2 cloves of garlic, sliced
- 1 head of tatsoi, pak choi or choi sum, leaves separated and stems roughly chopped

TO SERVE:
- steamed rice (60–75g/2¼–2¾oz uncooked white rice per person)
- sliced red chillies, spring onions

1. Add a splash of oil to a large pan over a medium heat. When hot, add the pork and brown lightly. Add the remaining ingredients, apart from the coconut water and eggs, and continue to cook, stirring, for a minute or two. Pour in the coconut water and bring to a simmer.

2. Meanwhile, make the caramel. Place a small pan over a medium heat, then add the sugar in an even layer and leave it to melt. When it starts to brown, tilt the pan, letting the caramel spread out so that all the sugar melts and is incorporated. When the caramel is a deep brown, but not burnt, carefully add the water, as it will bubble up dramatically. If the sugar sets, don't worry. Remove from the heat and pour (or scrape) the caramel into the pork broth. Mix well.

3. Simmer the pork, partially covered with a lid, for 1¼ hours, or until the meat is tender (stir occasionally and keep an eye on the liquid levels). Spoon the fat off the top of the broth towards the end of cooking.

4. About 20 minutes before the pork is ready, boil 4 eggs in a pan of simmering water for 7 minutes. Cool in chilled water, then peel and set aside.

5. At the same time, prepare the greens: place a splash of oil in a pan over a medium heat. When hot, add the garlic and sauté for 1 minute. Add the tatsoi stems and leaves, season with salt

and add a splash of water, toss well, then cover the pan and steam for a couple of minutes, or until wilted. Remove from the heat and keep warm.

6. A couple of minutes before you're ready to serve, place the whole peeled eggs in the broth to warm through and absorb some of the flavour. Taste the broth and add a final teaspoon of the fish sauce if it needs a bit more umami to cut through the sweetness.

7. Serve the pork and broth in bowls, with the rice and drained garlicky greens, and the eggs halved and on top. Sprinkle with sliced spring onions and red chillies just before tucking in.

Spicy Pork Meatballs

Tender pork meatballs with lime leaf and chilli, in a spicy coconut curry. If you're short on time – or culinary energy – you can make the curry with a good quality Thai curry paste instead.

PREP TIME 25 MINUTES • COOK TIME 30 MINUTES

NF • SERVES 4

- 500g (1lb 2oz) minced pork, with 10–20% fat
- 6 lime leaves, very finely chopped
- 3 spring onions, very finely chopped
- 2 red chillies, very finely chopped
- 3 cloves of garlic, crushed
- 2 tablespoons panko breadcrumbs
- 1 teaspoon freshly grated ginger
- 1 teaspoon miso paste
- 1 teaspoon fish sauce
- oil, for cooking
- salt and freshly ground black pepper

FOR THE CURRY SAUCE:
- 1 onion, finely sliced
- 2 cloves of garlic, crushed
- 1 stick of lemongrass, tougher outer layer discarded, cut into 3 pieces
- 1 red chilli, finely chopped
- 1 teaspoon each ground turmeric, cumin and coriander
- ½ teaspoon chilli powder, or to taste
- 1 × 400ml (14fl oz) can full-fat coconut milk
- 400ml (14fl oz) hot chicken stock
- 2 teaspoons fish sauce, plus extra to taste
- 6 lime leaves, torn
- 125g (4½oz) green beans, halved

TO SERVE:
- rice noodles or steamed jasmine rice
- Thai basil leaves, sliced red chillies and lime wedges

1. Place all the pork ingredients, except the oil, in a bowl and use your hands to massage them together. When thoroughly mixed, add a splash of cooking oil to a frying pan over a medium heat and fry a small piece of the pork to check the seasoning. When you're happy with the flavour, shape the rest of the mixture into 12 equal meatballs and gently pan-fry, turning regularly, until cooked through, about 10–12 minutes. (Cut one open to check that the juices run clear and no pink meat remains.)

2. While the meatballs brown, make the curry sauce. Place a large, heavy-based pan over a medium heat and add a splash of oil. Add the onion and a pinch of salt and sauté for 5 minutes. Add the garlic, lemongrass, chopped chilli, the spices and some black pepper. Cook for 1 minute, tossing to toast the spices. Add the coconut milk, stock, fish sauce and lime leaves and bring to a simmer. Cook for at least 10 minutes, or leave to simmer until the meatballs are cooked. Just before serving, remove and discard the lemongrass and lime leaves and add the meatballs and green beans. Cook for 2–3 minutes, or until the beans are just tender. If the curry sauce seems thick, add a little hot water. Taste and add more fish sauce if extra salt is needed.

3. Serve in wide bowls over rice noodles, or with steamed rice, garnished with Thai basil leaves and sliced chillies, and lime wedges on the side.

Berbere-Baked Chicken
with Red Lentils & Sweet Greens

Berbere is a vibrant spice blend used in Eritrean and Ethiopian cooking. It often contains chilli, coriander, cardamom, ginger, ajwain, nigella and – perhaps most importantly – fenugreek, which imparts a tangy, burnt sugar, slightly bitter flavour. Buy a good quality mixture and store it away from light and heat to extend its flavourful life. It works beautifully as a marinade for most meats, mixed with a little oil, especially chops, and in stews like doro wot (chicken) or siga wot (beef). Or you could try adding a pinch of it to hummus or to bean and lentil dishes.

PREP TIME 30 MINUTES + MARINATING • COOK TIME 45 MINUTES

SoF / NF / WF / GF • SERVES 4

- 2 tablespoons berbere spice blend
- 2 teaspoons paprika
- 3 tablespoons olive oil
- 1 tablespoon freshly squeezed lemon juice
- ½ teaspoon fine salt
- 8 chicken thighs
- 400g (14oz) basmati rice

FOR THE LENTILS:
- 150g (5½oz) red lentils
- 500ml (18fl oz) chicken or vegetable stock
- 1 tablespoon butter
- 1 tablespoon olive oil
- ½ onion, finely diced
- 3cm (1¼in) piece of ginger, peeled and finely grated
- 2 cloves of garlic, crushed or finely grated
- 1 teaspoon berbere spice blend
- 1 teaspoon paprika
- 1 tablespoon tomato purée
- salt and freshly ground black pepper

1. Place the spices, oil, lemon juice and salt in a bowl and stir to form a rough paste. Add the chicken and use your hands to massage the paste into the skin and meat. While it can be cooked straight away, it improves if covered and marinated in the fridge for at least 30 minutes, but ideally overnight.

2. Heat the oven to 200°C/425°F/gas mark 7. Line a baking tray with nonstick baking paper.

3. Place the chicken on the prepared tray and roast for 30 minutes.

4. Meanwhile, place the rice in a large saucepan and add enough water to come about 1cm (½in) above it. Bring to the boil, then turn the heat right down, cover and cook for 12 minutes. Fluff with a fork, cover again and set aside until needed.

5. While the rice and chicken cook, place the lentils in a pan and cover with the stock. Bring to a simmer, then cover and cook for about 15 minutes.

6. At the same time, melt the butter into the oil in a third pan over a medium heat. Gently sauté the onion for 6–8 minutes, until translucent but not browning (turn the heat to low if necessary). Add the ginger, garlic, berbere, paprika and tomato purée, and cook, stirring, for a minute or so. As soon

FOR THE GREENS:
- 2 knobs of butter
- a splash of olive oil
- ½ onion, finely diced
- 1 clove of garlic, crushed or finely grated
- 2cm (¾in) piece of ginger, peeled and finely grated
- 150g (5½oz) spring greens, ribs removed, leaves finely shredded (discard any that are tough or very thick)

TIP

Berbere often contains salt, so check yours and dial back the salt in the recipe, if necessary – you can always add more later.

as the mixture starts to brown and stick, add 1–2 spoonfuls of water and use it to loosen anything stuck to the base of the pan. Scrape this mixture into the lentil pan and stir together, adding a splash of water if it looks at all dry. Cover again and cook for a further 10–15 minutes, or until the lentils are collapsing into the broth and no longer feel gritty. Season well with salt and black pepper. Keep warm.

7. For the greens, melt a knob of the butter into the oil in a clean pan over a medium heat. Gently sauté the onion until translucent, then add the garlic and ginger. Cook for 1 minute, then add the greens, turn the heat to low and cover with a lid. Leave to steam for about 8 minutes; finish by stirring in the final knob of butter and some black pepper.

8. Remove the chicken from the oven and set aside to rest for a few minutes; keep warm.

9. Serve the chicken on top of a mound of fluffy rice, with the lentil stew and greens on the side. Make sure you scoop up every last bit of the spicy chicken juices and spoon them over the meat and rice.

→ *Pictured overleaf*

Saltfish & Plantain Fritters
with Spicy Ackee

Scotch bonnet chillies pack a punch, but we reckon you can handle it. (Remember to wash your hands after touching them, or handle with gloves.) The plantain flesh binds the fritters without eggs or milk – usually, you might make either plantain fritters or saltfish fritters, but combining the two creates light, salty and very crisp little balls of deliciousness.

PREP TIME 30 MINUTES • COOK TIME 1¼ HOURS

SoF / NF / DF • SERVES 4

- 350g (12oz) saltfish
- 1 ripe plantain, with lots of brown spots on it
- 1 teaspoon baking powder
- 75g (2¾oz) plain flour
- 3 spring onions, finely chopped
- ½ green pepper, finely chopped
- ½ teaspoon paprika
- ½ teaspoon garlic powder
- 1 teaspoon fresh thyme leaves
- 1 tablespoon finely chopped flat leaf parsley
- ¼ teaspoon freshly ground black pepper
- 100ml (3½fl oz) water
- neutral oil, for cooking

TIP

Many of the larger supermarkets sell preserved saltfish, ackee and plantains.

1. Rinse the salt fish under cold running water, then place in a saucepan and cover with cold water. Bring to the boil, then cover and simmer for 20 minutes. Pour out the water, rinse the fish and pan, refill with fresh water (you can use hot water from the kettle this time) and bring back to the boil. Simmer for a further 15–20 minutes. Use a fork to break off a piece of fish and taste it. It will still be a little salty, but not overpoweringly so. If it is still very salty, repeat the simmering process.

2. While the fish simmers, peel the plantain, chop the flesh into chunks and mash thoroughly (it will be firmer than a banana, even though they look similar).

3. Drain and flake the fish, discarding any bones and skin, and add the flesh to the plantain. Add all the other fritter ingredients, except the oil, and mix thoroughly.

4. Heat the oven to its lowest temperature. Pour a 3cm (1¼in) depth of cooking oil into a frying pan over a medium–high heat. When hot, add a nugget of the fish mixture, fry until golden, then taste. The mixture won't need more salt, but you can add more of the other herbs and spices, if you like.

5. Divide the mixture into 16 equal pieces and flatten into patties about 2cm (¾in) thick. Cook a few at a time in the

FOR THE SPICY ACKEE:
- 1 onion, finely chopped
- ½ red pepper, diced
- ½ yellow pepper, diced
- 6 ripe cherry tomatoes, seeds removed, diced
- 2 cloves of garlic, crushed
- 1 spring onion, finely chopped
- ½ Scotch bonnet chilli pepper, seeds removed, very finely diced (about 1 teaspoon)
- 1 teaspoon fresh thyme leaves
- a pinch of ground allspice
- 1 × 540g (1lb 3oz) can cooked ackee in water, drained
- salt and freshly ground black pepper

TO SERVE:
- sliced avocado, coriander leaves, lime wedges, mayo or garlic mayo, hot sauce, or mayo mixed with hot sauce

hot oil for 3–4 minutes on each side, until golden and crisp. Drain on a plate lined with kitchen paper and keep warm in a low oven.

6. Now make the spicy ackee. Place the onion, peppers, a splash of oil and a pinch of salt in a wide pan set over a medium heat. Fry until the onions begin to soften, then add the tomatoes, garlic, spring onion and Scotch bonnet. Cook for a couple of minutes, then add the thyme, allspice and some black pepper, and cook for another minute or so, stirring to distribute the flavours. Spoon the ackee into the pan and stir very gently once or twice, just to warm it through, and being careful not to break it up too much.

7. Serve the warm fritters with the ackee on the side, plus some sliced avocado, coriander leaves, lime wedges and your choice of mayo and hot sauce.

→ *Pictured overleaf*

Crispy Gochujang Tofu

Gochujang is a Korean chilli paste that is sweet, hot and very savoury, meaning it works brilliantly to liven up dishes made with creamy tofu and steamed rice. Find it in larger supermarkets.

PREP TIME 25 MINUTES • COOK TIME 35 MINUTES
NF / DF / V / Ve • SERVES 4

- 300g (10½oz) uncooked Japanese short-grain (sushi) rice
- 450ml (16fl oz) cold water
- 450g (1lb) extra-firm tofu, cut into 2.5cm (1in) cubes
- 2 teaspoons soy sauce
- 2 teaspoons sesame oil
- 1½ tablespoons cornflour
- 1–2 tablespoons neutral oil
- salt

FOR THE SAUCE:
- 2 tablespoons gochujang (Korean chilli paste)
- 1 tablespoon agave nectar (or honey if Ve not an issue)
- 1 teaspoon rice wine vinegar
- 1 tablespoon sesame oil
- 2 teaspoons lime juice

TO GARNISH:
- 3 spring onions, finely sliced
- toasted black or white sesame seeds

1. Rinse the rice, then place it in a large pan with a pinch of salt. Pour in the water, cover and bring to a simmer. Turn the heat to medium–low and cook for 20 minutes. Fluff up the rice with a fork, cover again and set aside for 10 minutes, or until needed.

2. Meanwhile, place the tofu in a bowl, add the soy sauce and sesame oil and toss to coat. After 10 minutes or so, add the cornflour and toss again – the soy sauce and cornflour will form a light batter around the tofu.

3. Pour a thin layer of vegetable oil into a large frying pan over a medium heat. When hot, add the tofu in a single layer and fry for 5–7 minutes without moving it (the cubes will stick at first). Once the underside is golden, turn using tongs and a spatula, and cook the other sides until golden brown and crisp. Drain on a plate lined with kitchen paper.

4. Meanwhile, whisk all the sauce ingredients together in a bowl. Add a splash of water if it feels quite thick; it should be spoonable, like runny honey. Taste to ensure it is sweet, spicy and with a bright sourness from the vinegar and lime.

5. Serve the tofu with the rice and the sauce, sprinkling each portion with some of the spring onions and sesame seeds.

SIDES
&
SAUCES

Emily's Cape Malay Pickled Fish

This is much loved by Emily-Jayne Wooding in LEON's grocery team. 'A South African favourite that goes down a treat in my family. This is my brother's recipe and is perfect as a side at a barbecue, always with freshly baked bread to mop up the sauce. Try to make it ahead to allow the fish to absorb the spices and pickle juice.'

PREP TIME 15 MINUTES • COOK TIME 20 MINUTES + CHILLING

SoF / NF / DF (CAN ALSO BE WF /GF) • SERVES 4 AS A SIDE

- 2 tablespoons olive oil
- ½ onion, sliced into rings
- 1 clove of garlic, crushed
- 1cm (½in) piece of ginger, grated
- 1 teaspoon mild curry powder
- ½ teaspoon ground turmeric
- ¼ teaspoon ground allspice
- ¼ teaspoon coriander seeds, toasted
- ¼ teaspoon ground cumin
- 250ml (9fl oz) white wine vinegar
- 75g (2¾oz) caster sugar
- 1 bay leaf
- 3 tablespoons plain flour (WF / GF if needed)
- 400g (14oz) sustainably caught skinless white fish, cut into roughly 5cm (2in) pieces
- salt and freshly ground black pepper

1. Add 1 tablespoon of the oil to a frying pan over a medium heat. When hot, sauté the onion for 3–4 minutes. Turn down the heat, add the garlic, ginger and all the spices, and fry for 2 more minutes.

2. Add the vinegar, sugar and bay leaf, stirring until the sugar dissolves, then simmer for 20 minutes until the onion is soft.

3. When the onion is almost done, pour a little plain flour into a wide bowl and mix in some salt and pepper. Dust the fish in the seasoned flour.

4. Heat the remaining tablespoon oil in a medium-sized, nonstick frying pan and fry the fish until golden but still tender.

5. Place half the fish in a non-metallic baking dish and cover it with half the onion mixture. Add the remaining fish and the remaining onion mixture. Allow to cool, then chill until you're ready to serve.

Sweet Yellow Coconut Rice

This beautiful sweet-savoury rice is great with Southeast Asian-inspired dishes, such as coconut-based seafood or fish curries, egg curry or fried chicken (if you want to serve it with Indian-style curries, see the Tip below).

PREP TIME 5 MINUTES • COOK TIME 20 MINUTES + STANDING

SoF / NF / WF / GF / DF / V / Ve • SERVES 4 AS A SIDE

- 250g (9oz) long-grain rice
- 250ml (9fl oz) water
- 250ml (9fl oz) coconut milk, from a well-shaken can
- 1 stick of lemongrass, bruised with a heavy-based pan
- 1 teaspoon ground turmeric
- 2 lime leaves
- 1 bay leaf
- fine salt

1. Place all the ingredients in a pan with a generous pinch of salt and stir well. Cover and bring to a simmer over a medium heat, then lower the heat and cook for 15 minutes.
2. Remove from the heat. Fluff up the rice with a fork – all the liquid should have been absorbed – then replace the lid and leave to stand for at least 10 minutes. Remove the aromatics just before serving.

TIP

To serve the rice with Indian dishes, omit the lemongrass and lime leaves. Sauté a crushed clove of garlic in a knob of butter before adding the rice and add a few curry leaves, 4 or 5 green cardamom pods, a couple of cloves, a pinch of cumin seeds and a small stick of cinnamon.

Bacon Dauphinoise

Although technically a side, we are very happy to eat this creamy layered potato bake as a main course, with a lemon-dressed salad of bitter leaves.

PREP TIME 20 MINUTES • COOK TIME 1¾ HOURS + STANDING

SoF / WF / GF • SERVES 4–6

- 500ml (18fl oz) double cream (lower-fat alternatives will split during cooking)
- 250ml (9fl oz) milk
- a pinch of freshly grated nutmeg
- scant ½ teaspoon fine salt and black or white pepper
- 4 cloves of garlic, crushed
- 1 teaspoon finely chopped fresh thyme and/or rosemary
- 850g (1lb 14oz) floury potatoes, such as Maris Piper, sliced as finely as possible (see Tip page 95; we leave the peel on for the extra nutrients, but it can be removed if you prefer)
- 4 smoked back bacon rashers, chopped or snipped into 2cm (¾in) pieces
- a splash of neutral oil, for cooking

1. Place the cream, milk, nutmeg, salt, pepper, garlic and thyme and/or rosemary in a large pan over a medium heat and bring almost to a simmer. Remove from the heat and add the potatoes in small batches, mixing to coat the slices thoroughly with the cream. Set aside for 10 minutes.

2. Meanwhile, fry the bacon in a little oil until crisp, then set aside.

3. Heat the oven to 160°C/350°F/gas mark 4. Set out a ceramic baking dish (about 30 × 20cm/12 × 8in).

4. Using tongs, transfer half the potatoes to the dish, leaving the cream in the pan for now. Scatter with the bacon pieces, leaving any fat behind, then cover evenly with the rest of the potatoes. Stir the cream mixture and pour it over the potatoes until they are just covered. Don't overfill the dish or it will boil over during cooking.

5. Place the dish on a rimmed baking tray in the hot oven and bake for 1–1¼ hours. When done, the top should be golden and the potatoes tender when pierced with the point of a knife. Cook for another 5–10 minutes if necessary, but cover the dish with foil if the top browns before the potatoes are done. Leave to stand for 10 minutes before serving.

⟶ *Pictured overleaf*

TIP

For anchovy dauphinoise, which goes beautifully with grilled fish and a green salad, swap the bacon for 6 anchovies in oil, drained and very finely chopped.

Smoky Spicy Potatoes

Serve these with grilled fish or meat, or with a crispy fried egg.

PREP TIME 10 MINUTES • **COOK TIME 18 MINUTES**

SoF / NF / WF / GF / DF / V /Ve • **SERVES 4 AS A SIDE**

- 500g (1lb 2oz) waxy potatoes, roughly chopped into bite-sized chunks
- 2 tablespoons olive oil
- 1 onion, finely sliced
- 3 cloves of garlic, crushed
- 1 teaspoon tomato purée
- ½ teaspoon smoked paprika
- a pinch of fennel seeds (optional)
- a pinch of red chilli flakes, or more, to taste
- salt and freshly ground black pepper
- roughly chopped parsley or coriander, to garnish
- aïoli or garlic mayonnaise, to serve

1. Cook the potatoes in a large pan of boiling salted water for 10 minutes. Drain.
2. Place a wide, heavy-based frying pan over a medium–high heat. Add the oil, then cook the onions on one side of the pan, and the potatoes on the other side. Allow both the onions and potatoes to brown, turning the potatoes so that they become golden all over, and moving the onions around to prevent burning, about 10–12 minutes. Add a pinch of salt to the onions. Turn the heat to low, add the garlic and tomato purée and cook, stirring everything together, for 3–4 minutes.
3. Add the smoked paprika, fennel seeds, if using, chilli flakes and a good twist of ground black pepper. Cook for another couple of minutes. If the pan starts to look very dry, add a splash of water to loosen; everything should look glossy, but not wet.
4. Serve garnished with the herbs, and offer the aïoli or garlic mayo to serve.

← *Pictured on previous pages*

Parmesan Smashed Potatoes

Our version of the TikTok recipe craze. OK, we were influenced, but with good reason.

PREP TIME 10 MINUTES • COOK TIME 45 MINUTES

SoF / NF / WF / GF / V • SERVES 4 AS A SIDE

- 500g (1lb 2oz) small, waxy potatoes, such as Charlotte
- 25g (1oz) salted butter
- 1 tablespoon olive oil
- 40g (1½oz) Parmesan cheese, finely grated (check V, if needed)
- a pinch of garlic powder
- 1 teaspoon finely chopped rosemary
- freshly ground black pepper

1. Cook the whole potatoes in a covered pan of boiling, salted water for about 10 minutes, or until just tender – they don't need to be fully cooked. Drain, then place on a board. Use the bottom of a mug to squash each one lightly, aiming to create thick, rough-edged rounds.

2. Heat the oven to 200°C/425°F/gas mark 7. When hot, put the butter and olive oil in a large roasting tray and heat until the fats are foaming and beginning to brown, about 5 minutes. Sprinkle evenly with a third of the Parmesan, the garlic powder, some black pepper and the rosemary. Carefully add the potatoes, turning them once in the hot, cheesy butter to coat well. Sprinkle with the remaining Parmesan, then roast for 25–35 minutes, or until the potatoes and cheese are golden and crisp.

3. Use tongs to lift out the potatoes, then drain on kitchen paper, if necessary. Scrape up the browned cheese left in the pan and drain that too. Transfer the potatoes to a serving bowl, sprinkle with the crunchy cheese and eat hot or warm.

← *Pictured on previous pages*

TIP

Serve with a dip as a nibble with drinks: mix 100ml (3½fl oz) soured cream with 2 tablespoons mayo, some black pepper, 1 finely chopped spring onion and a handful of finely chopped chives and parsley.

Mariam's Green Mustard

*'This is one of my go-tos when I have a barbecue,' says Mariam French,
LEON's marketing director. 'I particularly love it with sausages — my favourite
are Eastern European-style smoky sausages, fresh off the grill.'*

PREP TIME 5 MINUTES • COOK TIME 0 MINUTES
SoF / NF / V / Ve • SERVES 4–6

- 100g (3½oz) American-style yellow mustard
- 50g (1¾oz) mizuna or rocket, roughly chopped

1. Place all the ingredients in a blender and blitz until completely smooth. Transfer to a bowl, then cover and store in the fridge. Use within 2–3 days.

Mariam's Spicy Bomb Sauce

*'Whenever you pop by my place for a bite, you'll always find a spread of condiments,'
says Mariam. 'I love this spicy sauce – it looks fantastic and also packs a punch.
It's very popular with my friends.'*

PREP TIME 5 MINUTES • COOK TIME 0 MINUTES
SoF / NF / WF / GF / DF / V • MAKES 1 × 400ML (14FL OZ) JAR

- 100g (3½oz) piquillo peppers from a jar, roughly chopped
- 2 tablespoons chilli paste (we love chipotle paste for this, but harissa paste also works brilliantly, as does smoked chilli paste)
- 4 tablespoons tomato purée
- 2 teaspoons honey
- 4 tablespoons mirin (sweet rice wine)
- 1 teaspoon soft brown sugar

1. Start by sterilizing a heatproof 400ml (14fl oz) glass jar with lid (see Tip, page 188).
2. Place all the ingredients in a blender and blitz until smooth. If very thick, add just enough water to make it a spoonable sauce. Transfer to the sterilized jar, seal tightly, then label and date.

Piri Piri Sauce

This is a recipe Rebecca collected when working on a cookbook in Lisbon.
The degree of heat can be tailored to your taste by altering the type or amount of chillies.
Use as a hot sauce, or as a marinade for chicken.

PREP TIME 15 MINUTES • COOK TIME 0 MINUTES

SoF / DF / V / Ve • MAKES 1 SMALL JAR

- 4 garlic cloves
- 4 tablespoons white wine vinegar
- 3 medium-hot, long red chilli peppers
- 3 piri piri, malagueta or African bird's eye chillies, or more to taste
- 2 red peppers
- 6 tablespoons olive oil
- 1 teaspoon fine salt
- 1 tablespoon lemon juice
- 1 teaspoon hot piri piri powder (optional, if your chillies are not very spicy)
- 2 tablespoons whisky

1. Start by sterilizing a 400g (14oz) heatproof glass jar and lid (see Tip, page 188).
2. Place all the ingredients in a blender and purée until roughly combined. Taste and decide whether you would like more heat; this sauce should be medium-hot, but add another chilli or even two if you really like spice. Purée until very smooth, then pour into your sterilized jar, label and date, and store in the fridge for up to a month.

Sambal Oelek

Sambal oelek (or ulek) is a really versatile hot sauce, originally from Indonesia. Try it on top of creamy curries or lentil dhals, with scrambled eggs, tofu or grilled meat, fish or roasted vegetables, in tacos or burritos ... or anywhere you want a flash of chilli fire.

PREP TIME 5 MINUTES • COOK TIME 0 MINUTES

SoF / NF / WF / GF / DF / V / Ve • MAKES 1 × 200ML (7FL OZ) JAR

- 200g (7oz) red chillies, roughly chopped
- 2 teaspoons rice wine vinegar
- 1 teaspoon fine salt

1. Place the chillies, vinegar and salt in a blender or small food processor. (Beware the chilli-mist that comes out of the blender after blitzing and keep your face away.) Blitz until you get a chunky purée, scraping down the sides once or twice. As they break down, the chillies will release a lot of liquid, so don't add water to help things along.

2. Cautiously taste the sauce. It should be really fiery, salty and a little bit sharp; adjust the salt and vinegar if necessary. When you're happy with the flavour, scrape it all into a sterilized jar or container, seal tightly, then label and date, and store in the fridge. This isn't fermented, but will keep for a week or more; use judiciously, as its heat may increase over time.

→ *Pictured on page 191*

TIP

Sterilize glass jars and their lids by placing them in a low oven for 15 minutes. Alternatively, wash them in hot soapy water, then rinse with boiling water and leave to air-dry.

Fermented Hot Sauce

Sour. Saucy. Alive! And with one heck of a kick.

PREP TIME 20 MINUTES + FERMENTING • COOK TIME 0 MINUTES

SoF / NF / WF / GF / DF / V / Ve • MAKES 350–400ML (12–14FL OZ)

- about 300g (10½oz) red chillies, washed in warm soapy water, rinsed then roughly chopped with stems, seeds and ribs removed
- about 100g (3½oz) long, sweet red peppers, washed in warm soapy water, rinsed then roughly chopped with stems, seeds and ribs removed
- 1 clove of garlic
- 8g (less than ¼oz) fine salt (or at least 2% of the weight of the prepared peppers – see method)
- 1–2 teaspoons cider vinegar

1. Start by sterilizing 2 × 400g (14oz) heatproof glass jars with lids, or a 1 litre (1¾ pint) preserving jar (see Tip, page 188).

2. Weigh the prepared chillies and peppers and calculate 2% of that figure to find the amount of salt required for the sauce to ferment safely without any nasty bugs taking hold. For example, 300g (10½oz) vegetables will need 6g of salt, while 400g (14oz) vegetables will need at least 8g. (We usually add about 2g extra to any figure to be on the safe side.)

3. Place the chillies, peppers, garlic and salt in a blender or food processor and blitz to a rough purée. Pour into the sterilized jars, making sure you have at least 4cm (1½in) of headspace at the top for any gases that might form (add a glass pickle weight now, if you have one). Seal the jars – loosely, if using screwtop ones – then label and date. Set aside somewhere cool and out of direct sunlight. Fermentation (indicated by bubbling) might take 24 hours in warm weather, or longer if your home is cool. Nonetheless, open the jars at least every 24 hours to release any gases. Keep tasting the sauce, using a clean spoon and never double-dipping (which introduces unwanted bacteria), until you're happy with the balance of sour, hot and salty flavours.

4. Now add the vinegar, starting with 1 teaspoon and tasting before deciding if you want more. The mixture can be left as it is, or blitzed until completely smooth. In either case, transfer to freshly sterilized jars, label and date again, and store in the fridge to halt fermentation. (If kept at room temperature, fermentation will continue and the jars could explode.)

↪ *Pictured on page 191*

TIP

Try a mixture of different peppers, such as habañero, jalapeño, ghost, Scotch bonnet or cherry, to amp up the heat, tang or sweetness. You could also use roasted fresh or rehydrated chillies, such as smoky chipotle or ancho, or try adding fresh onion or tomato purée.

Miso Mayo

Is there anything that doesn't taste better with a little miso added? We came up with this as a dipping sauce for crispy chicken, but you can also try it in burgers and wraps, or just plunge your fries into it.

PREP TIME 5 MINUTES • COOK TIME 0 MINUTES

NF / WF / GF / DF / V / Ve • MAKES ENOUGH FOR 4 BURGERS

DEPENDING ON MAYO USED • OR PORTIONS OF FRIES

- 3 heaped tablespoons mayonnaise
- 1 tablespoon white miso
- optional extras: freshly squeezed lime juice, freshly grated ginger or a small clove of very well-crushed garlic

1. Stir the mayo and miso together, ensuring no lumps remain. If very thick, add a dash of water to thin it out. This will keep for 3-4 days, covered and in the fridge.

TIP

If you fancy something sweet, sour, salty and a little spicy too, blitz some finely chopped pickled sushi ginger into the miso mayonnaise.

Pink Kraut

We serve a version of this tangy, bright pink, slow-fermented kraut on top of many of our salads and rice boxes. (Don't be tempted to reduce the salt – you need at least 2% of the cabbage's weight in salt to make sure it ferments safely.)

PREP TIME 20 MINUTES + FERMENTING • COOK TIME 0 MINUTES

NF / WF / GF / DF / V / Ve • MAKES 1 LITRE (1¾ PINT) JAR

- 1 small white cabbage (about 800g /1lb 12oz), stems and core removed, leaves very finely shredded
- 1 tablespoon fine sea salt
- 1 small beetroot, peeled and shredded (wear clean rubber gloves if you don't want to stain your hands, or wash your hands well immediately after this prep)
- 1 clove of garlic, finely chopped
- ½ teaspoon ground cumin
- ½ teaspoon ground coriander
- ½ teaspoon freshly ground black pepper
- 6 whole cloves (optional)
- 3 whole cardamom pods
- pinch of ground cinnamon (optional)

1. Place the cabbage in a bowl with the salt and beetroot. Massage the salt into the vegetables for a couple of minutes, until everything feels quite wet; this is the pickle's brine. Add the garlic and spices and mix well.

2. Using clean spoons or tongs, place the kraut mixture in a sterilized 1 litre (1¾ pint) glass jar, or two smaller ones (see Tip, page 188) and pour in all the brine. Top with a glass pickle weight or two, or a metal weight in a sandwich bag, to press the veg below the level of the brine, as anything above it might go mouldy over time. Seal the jar(s), making sure there is about 4cm (1½in) of headspace at the top, then label and date.

3. Store somewhere out of direct sunlight for 24 hours. Fermentation (indicated by bubbling) might take 24 hours in warm weather, or more if your home is cool. Nonetheless, open the jar(s) every day to release any gases. Taste, using a clean spoon and never double-dipping (which introduces unwanted bacteria). When you're happy with the balance of tart and sour flavours, transfer to the fridge to halt fermentation. As long as you always use clean spoons, the kraut should keep in the fridge for a couple of months.

1. Pink Kraut *page 192*
2. Fermented Kimchi *page 194*
3. Quick Pickles *page 195*

Fermented Kimchi

*First developed for our cookbook 'Happy Guts', this recipe has since had a few small tweaks –
we still love it. While it's not traditional to add carrot and turnip, Rebecca has been making
kimchi with them for years, and loves the sweet and peppery crunch they bring to it.*

PREP TIME 12 MINUTES • COOK TIME 15 MINUTES + FERMENTING

NF / WF / GF / DF / V / Ve • MAKES 1 LITRE (1¾ PINT) JAR

- 60g (2¼oz) non-iodized rock or sea salt
- 1 litre (1¾ pints) cold water
- 1 head of Chinese leaves, or ¼ head
  of white cabbage, cored and leaves
  roughly chopped
- 4cm (1½in) piece of ginger
- 8 cloves of garlic
- 3 tablespoons fish sauce (or soy sauce
  if V / Ve needed)
- 1 tablespoon soy sauce (WF / GF
  if needed)
- 1 teaspoon hot chilli flakes
- 3 teaspoons mild chilli powder (if you have
  Korean chilli powder, gochugaru, you will
  probably want 4–5 teaspoons, as it's fairly
  mild and gives traditional kimchi its
  red colour)
- 2 teaspoons paprika (omit if using
  gochugaru)
- 1 × 225g (8oz) mooli, peeled and cut into
  thin matchsticks
- 3 spring onions, cut into 1cm (½in) pieces
  on an angle (discard any green parts that
  can't be washed clean)
- 2 carrots, cut into matchsticks (optional)
- 1 small turnip, cut into matchsticks
  (optional)

1. Mix 25g (1oz) of the salt with the cold water in a large bowl,
   stirring until dissolved. Wash the cabbage in the salted water,
   then add the remaining salt and massage it into the leaves.
   Place the bowl in the fridge for at least for 6 hours, but ideally
   overnight, turning the leaves once or twice.

2. When ready to jar the kimchi, sterilize a 1 litre (1¾ pint)
   preserving jar or heatproof glass jar with lid (see Tip, page
   188). Place the ginger, garlic, fish sauce, soy sauce, chilli flakes,
   chilli powder and paprika into a blender or food processor and
   blitz to a paste. If it's too dry to blitz, add a tablespoon or two
   of water. If you don't have a processor, chop everything finely
   and pound to a paste with a pestle and mortar.

3. Drain the salted cabbage and rinse well in clean running
   water, then rinse it in two changes of clean water, massaging it
   again to work any remaining salt out of its crevices. Drain well.

4. Return the rinsed cabbage to a large bowl, add the rest of the
   vegetables, then pour in the ginger-garlic purée. Use a spoon,
   tongs or gloved hands to work the purée into the vegetables
   until well coated, then spoon it all into your sterilized jar.
   Press the kimchi down with the back of a spoon, making sure
   there is 3–5cm (1¼–2in) headspace above it (add a glass pickle
   weight now, if you have one). Seal the jar, then label and date,
   and leave to ferment at a steady room temperature out of
   direct sunlight. Fermentation (indicated by bubbling when
   you release the lid or tap the jar) might take 24 hours in warm
   weather, or up to 5 days if your home is cool. Whatever the

case, release the lid at least once every 24 hours to allow any fermenting gases to escape. Press the kimchi back down into the brine with a clean spoon, then reseal (or, if your jar has a screw-top lid, leave it loose).

5. Once the kimchi has started fermenting, transfer it to the fridge for at least a week, preferably two, as the flavours will continue to develop. The longer you leave it, the tangier the kimchi will become. It will keep for up to a couple of months, as long as you always use clean spoons to serve or taste it, and make sure to press down the vegetables so that they are always covered with brine.

← *Pictured previous pages*

Quick Pickles

Previously published in 'Happy Guts', the pickles below are too useful not to include here as well. The brine is enough for two jars, so either make one jar of each, or double the quantity of your favourite.

PREP TIME 15 MINUTES • COOK TIME 5 MINUTES

SoF / NF / WF / GF / DF / V / Ve • MAKES 2 × 400G (14OZ) JARS

- 135ml (4½fl oz) white wine vinegar
- 3 tablespoons cider vinegar
- 5½ tablespoons water
- 1½ teaspoons caster sugar
- 1½ teaspoons fine salt

FOR PINK PICKLED ONIONS:
- 1 red onion, very finely sliced

FOR PICKLED RADISHES:
- 150g (5½oz) radishes, cut into 4 or 6 pieces
- 2 cloves of garlic, sliced

1. Start by sterilizing 2 × 400g (14oz) heatproof glass jars with lids (see Tip page 188). Set aside.
2. To make the brine, place the vinegars, water, sugar and salt in a non-reactive (stainless steel or enamel-coated) pan. Bring to the boil, then set aside.
3. Meanwhile, pack the vegetables tightly into the prepared jars. Pour in the hot brine, immediately seal the jars, then label and date. Store them somewhere dark and cool.
4. The onions can be used as soon as they're cool, but all pickles are better if left for at least a few days to develop. Once open, store in the fridge and use a clean spoon every time you dip in.

← *Pictured previous pages*

7

SWEET
THINGS

Chilli & Sour Cherry Brownies

Spicy chocolate might sound unusual, but mixing chocolate with chilli has a history stretching back around 3,500 years, to the Mayans, Olmecs and Aztecs (eating or drinking cacao was recently found to date as far back as 5,300 years, to the Mayo-Chinchipe people in Ecuador).

PREP TIME 15 MINUTES • COOK TIME 25 MINUTES

V • MAKES 12

- 75g (2¾oz) butter (or DF alternative if needed)
- 50ml (2fl oz) very mild olive oil
- 125g (4½oz) caster sugar
- 75g (2¾oz) dark chocolate (at least 70% cocoa solids), broken into pieces
- 2 eggs, plus 1 egg white
- ½ teaspoon fine salt
- 75g (2¾oz) light brown sugar
- 40g (1½oz) cocoa powder
- 75g (2¾oz) plain flour (WF / GF if needed)
- ½ teaspoon baking powder
- 1 teaspoon vanilla extract
- 50g (1¾oz) finely chopped nuts (optional) – peanuts work brilliantly, but almonds, hazelnuts, walnuts, pecans or brazils are also good
- 50g (1¾oz) dried sour cherries, or any dried fruit, chopped if large
- 1 teaspoon chilli flakes
- ¼ teaspoon chilli powder
- zest of ½ unwaxed lime (see Tip, page 82)
- 25g (1oz) good-quality milk chocolate (at least 40% cocoa solids, or DF alternative if needed), chopped into small pieces

1. Heat the oven to 170°C/375°F/gas mark 5. Line a 20 × 30cm (8 × 12in) baking tray with nonstick baking paper, allowing it to overhang the sides by 5cm (2in).

2. Place the butter, oil and caster sugar in a heatproof bowl and melt in the microwave, or over a saucepan of barely simmering water. Set aside to cool a little, then add the dark chocolate to the butter mixture and stir until completely melted.

3. In a separate bowl, whisk the eggs and egg white with the salt and brown sugar until pale, thick and mousse-like.

4. Combine the cocoa powder, flour and baking powder in a third bowl, then sift them over the whisked eggs, without mixing. Pour in the melted chocolate and vanilla extract, add the nuts, if using, the dried fruit, chilli flakes and chilli powder and the lime zest. Fold everything together until just combined. Pour into the lined tray and stud the top with the milk chocolate. Bake for 15 minutes for fudgy brownies, or 20–25 minutes if you prefer them more cake-like. Set aside to cool completely in the tray before slicing into 12 portions.

Blueberry Blondies

Inspired by our much-loved blueberry and yuzu blondies.

PREP TIME 20 MINUTES • COOK TIME 30 MINUTES

V • MAKES 15

- 200g (7oz) salted butter (or DF alternative, if needed)
- 150g (5½oz) soft light brown sugar
- 150g (5½oz) caster sugar
- 200g (7oz) good-quality white chocolate (or DF alternative, if needed)
- 250g (9oz) plain flour (WF / GF if needed)
- ½ teaspoon baking powder
- ¼ teaspoon fine salt
- 3 eggs, beaten
- 1 teaspoon vanilla extract
- zest of 1 unwaxed grapefruit (see Tip, page 82)
- 25g (1oz) pecans, chopped into small pieces (optional)
- 75g (2¾oz) blueberries

1. Heat the oven to 200°C/425°F/gas mark 7. Line the bottom and sides of a 20cm (8in) square baking tray with nonstick baking paper, allowing it to overhang the sides by 5cm (2in).

2. Place the butter and both sugars in a heatproof bowl and melt in the microwave or over a pan of barely simmering water. Once melted, break 100g (3½oz) of the chocolate into the bowl and stir until that melts too. Set aside to cool slightly.

3. Combine the flour, baking powder and salt in a large bowl.

4. When the butter has cooled enough that it won't cook the eggs, add them to the chocolate bowl along with the vanilla extract and grapefruit zest and mix thoroughly. Pour into the flour bowl and mix to form a batter. Now add the chopped pecans, if using.

5. Pour the batter into the prepared tray. Dot the top with the blueberries, pressing them down gently, but not fully submerging. Chop the remaining 100g (3½oz) white chocolate into little pieces and press them halfway into the batter too.

6. Bake for 30 minutes, until it has a slight wobble if you shimmy the tray. Set aside for 20–30 minutes, then use the paper to lift it out and transfer to a board. Cut into 15 portions. Eat warm, or freeze for later.

Cinnamon Cardamom Buns

Why choose between sticky-sweet cinnamon buns and perfumed cardamom buns when you could have both?

PREP TIME 30 MINUTES + PROVING/RISING • COOK TIME 40 MINUTES

SoF / NF / V • MAKES 12

- 250ml (9fl oz) milk
- 75g (2¾oz) butter, chopped
- 400g (14oz) strong white bread flour (WF / GF if needed)
- 100g (3½oz) plain flour, plus extra for dusting (WF / GF if needed)
- 100g (3½oz) caster sugar
- 1 tablespoon fast-action dried yeast
- seeds from 20 green cardamom pods, ground to a powder (see Tip page 115)
- 1½ teaspoons fine salt
- 2 eggs, beaten in separate bowls
- neutral oil, for greasing
- demerara sugar, for sprinkling

FOR THE FILLING:
- 100g (3½oz) salted butter
- 50g (1¾oz) caster sugar
- 2 tablespoons soft brown sugar
- 2 teaspoons ground cinnamon
- seeds from 20 green cardamom pods, ground to a powder

1. Warm the milk and butter in a small pan. Once the butter has melted, set aside until just warm.

2. Place the two flours in a large bowl with the sugar, yeast, ground cardamom and salt. Add the warm milk and one of the beaten eggs. Stir to form a sticky dough, then knead on a clean, lightly oiled surface for about 5 minutes, until smooth and stretchy. (If you prefer, the mixing and kneading can be done in a mixer.)

3. Oil a clean bowl and put the dough in it. Cover with a damp tea towel or clingfilm and leave in a warm place to rise for about 1 hour, or until doubled in size.

4. Meanwhile, place all the filling ingredients in a small bowl or pan and melt in a microwave or over a very low heat until just liquified. Stir well and set aside.

5. When the dough has risen, thoroughly flour a clean work surface. Line two large rimmed baking trays with nonstick baking paper, letting it overhang the sides.

6. Tip the dough onto the floured surface, knock out the air, then use a rolling pin to stretch and flatten it into a 35 × 50cm (14 × 20in) rectangle, with a short side nearest you. Spread the lower half of the dough with all but 2 spoonfuls of the butter filling. Fold the upper half of the dough over the filling, pressing to seal the edges, then roll it out again to roughly 30 × 45cm (12 × 18in). Add more flour to the surface if it gets sticky.

7. With a long side nearest you, use a sharp knife to cut the dough from top to bottom into 12 roughly 2.5cm (1in) wide

strips. Then cut the remaining dough into 6 thinner strips. Halve each of the thinner strips. In total you should have 12 thicker strips and 12 shorter, thinner strips. Take one of the thicker, longer strips and twist it to form a long loose spiral – it will stretch as you do so. Tie the dough strip into a loose single knot, tucking the loose ends in underneath. Take a shorter strip and wrap it over the knot, again tucking the loose ends out of sight beneath the bun. Place on the baking tray and continue until you have 12 buns. Place the trays somewhere warm for the buns to prove for 20–30 minutes.

8. When ready to bake, heat the oven to 180°C/400°F/gas mark 6. Brush the top of the buns with the remaining beaten egg and bake for 20 minutes. Remove from the oven and brush the buns again with the remaining cinnamon butter and sprinkle with a little demerara sugar. Turn the trays around as you return them to the oven so that the buns brown evenly. Bake for a further 10–20 minutes, until risen, firm to the touch and deep golden brown all over. Leave to cool slightly before eating. These are best eaten the day they are made, or frozen as soon as they're cool.

↪ *Pictured overleaf*

Chocolate Almond Biscotti

Biscotti are double-baked cookies, so are very crunchy and keep very well. The sweet almond flavour really stands out, offset by the bitterness of a dark chocolate drizzle.

PREP TIME 25 MINUTES • COOK TIME 40 MINUTES

SoF / V • MAKES ABOUT 30

- 100g (3½oz) whole almonds (skin on), roughly chopped
- 200g (7oz) plain flour (WF / GF if needed)
- 25g (1oz) ground almonds
- 2 teaspoons baking powder
- 175g (6oz) soft dark brown sugar
- a pinch of fine sea salt
- 2 eggs, beaten
- zest of 1 small unwaxed orange (see Tip, page 82)
- 1 teaspoon vanilla extract
- ½ teaspoon almond extract
- 100g (3½oz) dark chocolate, broken into small pieces (SoF if needed)

1. Heat the oven to 200°C/425°F/gas mark 7. Line two baking trays with nonstick baking paper.

2. Spread the chopped almonds over one of the trays, then place in the oven for 4 minutes, until lightly toasted and fragrant.

3. Place all the dry ingredients in a bowl with the almonds. Beat the eggs in a separate bowl with the orange zest, vanilla and almond extracts, then add to the dry ingredients. Mix first with a spoon, then your hands to create a firm but sticky dough. Divide it into two equal pieces, place one on each baking tray and shape into flattish logs about 20cm (8in) long, 8cm (3¼in) wide and 2 cm (¾in) thick. Bake for 20 minutes, turning the trays halfway through for even baking. Set aside to cool for 5 minutes. Turn the oven down to 160°C/375°F/gas mark 4.

4. Slice each log widthways into strips 1.5cm (½in) wide. Use a palette knife to arrange them on their side on the baking trays. Return to the oven for 10 minutes, then turn each biscuit and bake for a further 5 minutes. Set aside to cool and crisp up.

5. Place two-thirds of the chocolate in a heatproof bowl and melt gently in the microwave or over a pan of barely simmering water. Once liquid, remove from heat, add the remaining chocolate and stir until completely melted. Put a piping bag fitted with a fine nozzle (or a sandwich bag with a corner cut off) inside a mug letting it overhang the sides, and fill it with the chocolate mixture. Place all the biscotti on one of the baking trays, not quite touching each other, and pipe zigzags of the chocolate over them. Leave until the chocolate has set. Eat with coffee, hot chocolate or a glass of sweet wine.

Grapefruit & Ginger Flapjacks

A twist on the lime and ginger flapjacks we have on the LEON menu.

PREP TIME 10 MINUTES • COOK TIME 40 MINUTES

SoF / WF / GF / V • MAKES ABOUT 20

- 300g (10½oz) unsalted butter, plus extra for greasing
- 75g (2¾oz) soft dark brown sugar
- 6 tablespoons golden syrup
- 1 teaspoon ground ginger
- zest of 1 pink unwaxed grapefruit (see Tip, page 82), and 4 tablespoons juice
- a pinch of salt
- 250g (9oz) jumbo rolled oats (GF if needed)
- 200g (7oz) porridge oats (GF if needed)
- 4 tablespoons chopped almonds or hazelnuts, or chopped mixed nuts

1. Heat the oven to 170°C/375°F/gas mark 5. Line a 20 × 30cm (8 × 12in) baking tray with nonstick baking paper, scrunching it up first to help it stay in place.

2. Place the butter, sugar, golden syrup, ground ginger, grapefruit zest and salt in a small pan over a medium heat and melt everything together, stirring to combine.

3. Add all the oats, the grapefruit juice and the nuts. Stir well to combine, then tip the mixture into the prepared baking tray. Use a spatula or the back of a wooden spoon to smooth the mixture out, pressing it down firmly.

4. Bake for 25 minutes (30 minutes if you prefer crunchy flapjacks). Cut into squares while still warm, then leave to cool in the tray before eating.

Gyulshah's Tahini Swirl Cake

Gyulshah Mintash is our assistant manager at the Brent Cross branch of LEON, and this is their deliciously nutty tahini cake.

PREP TIME 20 MINUTES • COOK TIME 25 MINUTES

SoF / NF / V • SERVES 8

- 5½ tablespoons sunflower oil, plus extra for greasing
- 100g (3½oz) plain flour
- 1 teaspoon baking powder
- 125g (4½oz) soft dark brown sugar
- 1 egg
- 100g (3½oz) Greek-style plain yoghurt
- 4 tablespoons light-roasted tahini (sesame paste)
- 2 tablespoons maple syrup
- fine salt

1. Heat the oven to 180°C/400°F/gas mark 6. Oil the inside of a loose-bottomed 20cm (8in) cake tin.

2. Place the flour, baking powder and a pinch each of the salt and sugar in a large bowl and whisk together.

3. Crack the egg into another bowl, then add the measured oil, yoghurt and remaining sugar. Beat together until smooth. Pour this mixture into the flour bowl and mix just until no lumps remain.

4. Pour the batter into the prepared tin. Mix the tahini with a pinch of fine salt and the maple syrup. If very thick, add a splash of water, just enough to make it pourable. Drizzle the tahini mixture in a spiral over the cake, then use the edge of a large metal spoon to lightly marble the tahini, working in the same direction as the spiral.

5. Bake the cake for 25 minutes, until it pulls away from the side of the tin, the top is golden and firm to the touch, and a skewer inserted into the middle comes out clean. Leave to cool in the tin before turning out.

Hazelnut Meringues
with Espresso Chocolate Sauce

Although posh-looking, these puds are a cinch to make. Simply halve all the quantities if want to make only six meringues, but it's worth making more, as any extras will keep in an airtight container and provide a bonus pudding with the leftover sauce on another day.

PREP TIME 20 MINUTES • COOK TIME 1¼ HOURS + COOLING

SoF / WF / GF / V • MAKES 12

- 50g (1¾oz) blanched/skinned hazelnuts
- 1 tablespoon demerara sugar
- 4 egg whites
- 200g (7oz) caster sugar
- 1 teaspoon unsweetened cocoa powder

FOR THE ESPRESSO CHOCOLATE
SAUCE AND TOPPING:
- 300ml (10fl oz) whipping or double cream
- 100g (3½oz) good-quality dark chocolate (at least 70% cocoa solids)
- 20g (¾oz) salted butter
- 1 tablespoon soft brown sugar
- 2 tablespoons strong, freshly brewed espresso (can be decaf), or very strong instant coffee

1. Place the hazelnuts in a spice grinder or small food processor and pulse briefly – you want a few chunky bits for texture. Transfer them to a small pan over a medium heat, toast until they smell fragrant, then add the demerara sugar. Stir and set aside.

2. Heat the oven to 160°C/350°F/gas mark 4. Line two baking trays with nonstick baking paper.

3. Place the egg whites in a clean bowl and whisk until they form soft peaks. Add a tablespoon of the caster sugar and whisk again; repeat this until about half the sugar is incorporated. After that, you can add it more quickly, but don't dump it on top of the whites or you will crush the air out. When ready, the meringue should cling to the whisk and hold its shape when lifted (you should even be able to hold the bowl upside-down over your head). Sift the cocoa powder over the meringue and add about half the nut mixture. Use a large metal spoon to swirl both through the mixture so that the cocoa leaves a marble-like trail in it; don't overmix.

4. Use the spoon to place 12 mounds of meringue on the baking trays, using the spoon to gently shape them into rough circles. Scatter over some more of the toasted nuts, then bake for 1 hour. Remove and leave to cool completely.

5. When ready to serve, make the sauce and topping. Reserve 2 tablespoons of the cream, then whip the rest into soft peaks.

Place the chocolate, butter and soft brown sugar in a heatproof bowl and gently melt in the microwave or over a pan of barely simmering water (don't let the water touch the base of the bowl); if overheated, the chocolate will become gritty. Add the reserved (unwhipped) cream and the espresso and mix until smooth. If the chocolate 'seizes' or splits and begins to look oily and lumpy, which sometimes happens when liquid is added to melted chocolate, add a tablespoon or two of boiling water and beat vigorously until silky smooth again.

6. Place a meringue on each plate, top with some whipped cream, then spoon over the warm chocolate sauce.

Miso Apple Tarte Tatin
with Vanilla Mascarpone

*The wonderfully inventive chef and food writer Ravinder Bhogal first turned us onto the idea of
using miso in the caramel of a tarte tatin – its intense savouriness plays neatly against the otherwise
sweet tart. Our product development manager Ollie Short devised the vanilla mascarpone pairing.*

PREP TIME 15 MINUTES + COOLING • COOK TIME 50 MINUTES

NF / V • SERVES 6–8

- 1 sheet ready-rolled all-butter puff pastry
- plain flour, for dusting
- 100g (3½oz) caster sugar
- 50g (1¾oz) butter
- 2 teaspoons miso paste
- 6 small eating apples, such as Cox's,
  peeled, cored and quartered
- 150g (5½oz) mascarpone cheese
- ½–1 teaspoon vanilla extract

1. For this brilliantly simple sweet-and-savoury tart, you will
   need a small, heavy-based ovenproof frying pan or shallow,
   cast-iron casserole dish, measuring 20–25cm (8–10in) across.
   Unroll the pastry on a lightly floured work surface and place
   a round plate on it that is 2–3cm (¾–1¼in) wider than your
   pan. Cut around the plate, then prick the pastry circle all over
   with a fork. Transfer to a board and place in the fridge.

2. Meanwhile, pour the sugar into the frying pan, spreading
   it out evenly, then place over a low–medium heat (higher
   if the pan is very heavy-based) and leave to caramelize,
   5–7 minutes. If it seems to be dissolving unevenly, you can
   shimmy and tilt the pan so the heat is directly under the
   unmelted areas, but don't stir yet.

3. Melt the butter in the microwave or a small pan, then whisk
   in the miso paste; this can be tricky as miso doesn't melt
   or emulsify very easily, so just keep going until it's fairly
   well combined.

4. Once the sugar has fully dissolved, remove the pan from the
   heat and stir in the miso-butter mixture – it may bubble up,
   so be careful.

5. Arrange the apple quarters, rounded side down, on top of the
   caramel in your ovenproof pan, starting with a ring around
   the perimeter, and tucking each piece tightly against the

Continued overleaf →

previous piece. When the pan is full of concentric apple circles, place it over a low–medium heat, bring the caramel back up to a simmer and cook for 10 minutes. Set aside to cool completely.

6. About 45 minutes before you want to serve the tart, heat the oven to 200°C/425°F/gas mark 7.

7. Drape the chilled pastry over the cooled fruit and tuck the edges down into the pan. Cut a 1cm (½in) slit in the centre of the pastry to allow steam to escape. Bake for 30 minutes. Set the pan aside and let the tart cool for just 5 minutes; any longer and there's a risk that the caramel will set and weld itself to the pan.

8. Meanwhile, put the mascarpone into a bowl and beat in some of the vanilla extract, tasting to decide if you want a stronger flavour and adding more as needed.

9. Before turning out the tart, put on a pair of oven gloves as the caramel will still be very hot, and carefully tilt the pan. If there is a lot of liquid in the bottom, carefully pour it into a small jug. Having too much liquid from particularly juicy apples will make the turned-out tart soggy on the bottom.

10. Place a serving plate over the pan and briskly invert it to turn out the tart.

11. Serve the tart warm, with the jug of any extra caramel sauce on the table, and a scoop of the cold vanilla mascarpone alongside each slice.

TIP

You probably don't need us to tell you this, but a scoop of vanilla ice cream, melting into the salty caramel, is also a winner with this tart.

Sour Raspberry Sorbet

Rebecca makes this for her kids, who love sorbet (Rebecca doesn't love the weird ingredients ready-made sorbet sometimes contains, though). If you have an ice cream maker, you can make this in it.

PREP TIME 20 MINUTES + CHILLING/FREEZING • COOK TIME 10 MINUTES

SoF / NF / WF / GF / DF / V / Ve • SERVES 6–8

- 175ml (6fl oz) boiling water
- 175g (6oz) caster sugar
- 700g (1lb 9oz) frozen raspberries

1. Place the water and sugar in a small pan over a medium heat and cook, stirring, until you have a clear, thin syrup. Set aside to cool completely. Exactly how much syrup you get depends on how much evaporates in the pan, but you should be left with a little more than the 225ml (8fl oz) needed here. (Leftovers can be stored in the fridge for a couple of weeks, and used in cocktails.)

2. Place the raspberries and 225ml (8fl oz) of the cooled syrup in a high-powered blender and blitz to a purée. Transfer to a plastic tub with a lid and freeze for 1 hour. Remove from the freezer, blitz again and freeze for another hour. Repeat this process, but this time freeze the sorbet for 3 hours.

3. Scrape into a lidded tub and leave in the freezer overnight or until ready to serve.

4. Allow to soften for 10–15 minutes before serving.

→ *Pictured overleaf*

Apple & Ginger Sorbet

After eating a ginger sorbet served alongside vegan apple crumble at a lovely country pub (the Cherry Tree Inn, near Henley), we really wanted to create our own.

PREP TIME 25 MINUTES + APPROX 9 HOURS FREEZING • COOK TIME 0 MINUTES

SoF / WF / GF / DF / V / Ve • SERVES 4–6

- 6 Granny Smith apples, peeled then grated coarsely and cores discarded
- 1 lemon, halved
- 6cm (2½in) piece of ginger, peeled and cut into matchsticks
- 1 teaspoon finely grated fresh ginger
- 225ml (8fl oz) boiling water
- 225g (8oz) caster sugar
- 4 tablespoons chopped hazelnuts
- honey or maple syrup, to serve

1. Line a small baking tray with nonstick baking paper, letting the paper overhang the sides.
2. Place the grated apple in a bowl, squeeze over a little lemon juice and toss to coat. Tip into the prepared tray and spread out thinly. Cover with another sheet of baking paper, then weight it down with a board or a couple of small plates. Transfer to the freezer for 3 hours.
3. Meanwhile, place the ginger matchsticks and boiling water in a heatproof jug and set aside to infuse.
4. Allow the frozen apple to soften for about 15 minutes, then spoon it into a powerful blender and discard the baking paper. Strain the ginger infusion, discarding the matchsticks. Add the sugar to the liquid, stirring until completely dissolved, then pour into the blender with the grated ginger. Blitz until completely smooth. Pour back into the baking tray and return to the freezer for 1 hour. Rough up the mixture with a fork and return it to the freezer for 3 hours. Allow to soften for about 15 minutes, then scrape it out of the tray, breaking it up, and into the blender again. Taste, adding more lemon juice if it seems too sweet. Blitz again until smooth, then scrape into a lidded container and freeze completely.
5. When you're ready to serve, allow the sorbet to soften slightly for 15–20 minutes. Meanwhile, place the hazelnuts in a small, dry pan over a medium heat and toast, stirring often, until they are fragrant. Remove from the heat and quickly pour in the honey or maple syrup and stir to coat. Serve the sorbet scattered with the sticky hazelnuts.

TIP

If you don't have a high-powered blender, then you can use an ice-cream machine instead for this sorbet.

Glossary

UK	US
Aubergine	Eggplant
Back bacon rasher	Slice of lean bacon, such as Canadian-style bacon
Baking paper	Parchment paper
Beef, stewing	Beef, boneless chuck
Beetroot	Beets
Brine	Pickling liquid or salt solution
Broad beans	Fava beans
Broccoli, sprouting	Broccoli, baby (broccolini)
Cabbage, white	Cabbage, green
Cavolo nero	Tuscan or black-leaf kale
Chinese leaves	Chinese greens
Cider vinegar	Apple cider vinegar
Clingfilm	Plastic wrap
Coconut, desiccated	Coconut, dry unsweetened
Coriander	Cilantro (but ground coriander)
Cornflour	Cornstarch
Courgette	Zucchini
Cream, double	Cream, heavy
Flour, plain	Flour, all-purpose
Full-fat milk/yoghurt	Whole milk/yoghurt
Golden syrup	Use light corn syrup
Jug	Liquid measuring cup
Linseeds	Flaxseed
Kitchen paper	Paper towels
Knob (of butter)	Pat (of butter)
Mangetout	Snow peas
Minced beef/lamb/pork	Ground beef/lamb/pork
Mooli	Daikon radish
Mushrooms, chestnut	Mushrooms, cremini
Pak choi	Bok choy
Passata	Tomato puree
Piping bag (with a nozzle)	Pastry bag (with a tip)
Porridge	Oatmeal
Porridge oats	Rolled oats
Prawns	Shrimp
Rapeseed oil	Canola oil
Rocket	Arugula
Shortcrust pastry, ready made	Pie crust, premade refrigerated
Spring greens	Collard greens
Spring onions	Scallions
Sugar, caster	Sugar, superfine
Tea towel	Dish towel
Tomato purée	Tomato paste
Yeast, fast-action dried	Yeast, active dry

Cook's Notes

Unless stated otherwise in the recipes:

Nutrition advice is not absolute. Please consult a qualified nutritionist if you require specialist advice.

Standard level spoon measurements are used in all recipes.
1 tablespoon = one 15ml spoon; 1 teaspoon = one 5ml spoon

All milk and yoghurt are full fat.

All butter is salted unless stated otherwise.

All eggs are medium and preferably free-range.

All vegetables (including garlic) are medium-sized and should be peeled or trimmed.

Peppers should be deseeded, though chillies may be left unseeded if you like extra heat.

Ginger needs to be peeled (easiest with a spoon).

All herbs and leaves should be washed and trimmed, as necessary.

All canned beans should be drained and rinsed before use.

Fine sea salt and freshly ground black pepper should be used wherever seasoning is required.

All Celsius oven temperatures are for a fan oven.
For a conventional oven, increase the temperature by 20°C.

This book includes dishes made with nuts and nut derivatives. It is advisable for readers with known allergic reactions to nuts and nut derivatives and those who may be potentially vulnerable to these allergies, to avoid dishes made with nuts and nut oils. It is also prudent to check the labels of pre-prepared ingredients for the possible inclusion of nut derivatives.

Vegetarians should look for the 'V' symbol on a cheese to ensure it is made with vegetarian rennet.

Not all soy sauce is gluten-free – we often use tamari, which is almost always gluten-free, but do check the label.

If you are cooking for someone with any known allergies, remember to check the labels on ready-made ingredients to ensure they don't contain allergens.

Index

Biographies & Acknowlegements

LEON

LEON was founded on the twin principles that food can both taste good and do you good. When Henry Dimbleby, John Vincent and Allegra McEvedy opened their first restaurant, on London's Carnaby Street in July 2004, their aim was to change the face of fast food. Six months after opening, LEON was named the Best New Restaurant in Great Britain at the *Observer Food Monthly* Awards (by a judging panel that included Rick Stein, Gordon Ramsay, Nigel Slater, Heston Blumenthal, Ruth Rogers and Jay Rayner). There are now almost 80 LEON restaurants in the UK and the Netherlands. LEON has published more than 20 cookbooks including *LEON Fast Vegan*, *LEON Happy Salads*, *LEON Happy Guts* and *LEON Happy One-pot Vegetarian*.

When we started LEON in 2004, our mission was simple – to make it easier for everyone to eat well with food that tastes good and does good for the planet. Fast forward to today, and we're still trying to shake things up in the world of fast food. This wouldn't be possible without a long list of amazing people.

First, hats off to our restaurant managers. These stars work tirelessly, bringing the warmth and sunshine of LEON to every guest. You're the heartbeat of LEON, making it all happen daily. Keep being awesome.

Next up, our incredible Copperfield Support Team. You're the silent heroes, ensuring everything runs smoothly behind the scenes. And a huge shoutout to our flavour explorers in the Food Team – Erica, Ollie, and Jo. Your tastebuds are legendary, and we're so happy to see your personal favourite recipes in this book.

To our guests, thank you for believing in us. Whether you're grabbing a meal at one of our restaurants, picking up something from our grocery range or enjoying one of our cookbooks, your support fuels our mission.

Finally, special thanks to our sunshine-filled author Rebecca and the wonderful team at Octopus. You make the dream of creating cookbooks a reality, and the process is always a joy.

That's a wrap. Another book down. We're truly grateful to everyone who helps us keep the mission alive – getting everyone to eat well and live well.

Rebecca Seal

Rebecca has written about food and drink for the *Observer*, the *Guardian*, the *Financial Times*, *Evening Standard*, *The Sunday Times*, *National Geographic* and *Sainsbury's Magazine*. Her cookbooks include *Istanbul: Recipes from the heart of Turkey*, *Lisbon: Recipes from the heart of Portugal* and *LEON Big Salads*, as well as co-authoring *LEON Happy Soups*, *LEON Happy One-pot Cooking*, *LEON Happy Curries*, *LEON Happy Fast Food* and *LEON Happy Guts* with John Vincent, *LEON Fast Vegan* with John Vincent and Chantal Symons, and *LEON Happy One-Pot Vegetarian* with Chantal Symons. Her first non-food book – *SOLO: How To Work Alone (And Not Lose Your Mind)* – was published in 2020, and *Be Bad Better: How Not Trying So Hard Will Set You Free* was published in 2023. She lives in London with her husband and two daughters.

Whenever we start a new LEON book, I still have to pinch myself that I get to do this as a job, that I continue to get to work with the brilliant team at LEON and that I can continue helping to create beautiful books. Thank you to Mariam, Ollie and Erica, and everyone else at LEON who gave me ideas and inspiration (and answered my annoying emails requesting overly precise recipe details).

Thanks to the fantastic shoot team who, once again, made the food look so very, very delicious: photographer Steven Joyce, food stylist Troy Willis and his assistant Jess Geddes and our amazing props stylist Rosie Jenkins – who sources the most covetable tableware imaginable – and Steve's assistants Rosie Alsop, Jordan Peck and Dimitrios Brouzioutis. (Special thanks to Troy in particular for noticing that I'd written a recipe for kimchi fritters ... containing no actual kimchi.)

Thank you to everyone at Octopus, especially Alison Starling, Pauline Bache, Jonathan Christie for all their hard work getting the book together, and then to Matt Grindon and Rosa Patel for all their hard work getting it in front of journalists, editors and, most importantly, readers. Thanks to my agent Antony Topping, as ever, for getting me here in the first place, and for patiently listening to me worry about deadlines on the phone.

I hope you enjoy this book – especially the kimchi fritters – as much as we loved making it.